UNDERGROUND

Official
Handbook

Bob Bayman

Capital Transport

ISBN 185414 221 6

Published by Capital Transport Publishing
38 Long Elmes, Harrow Weald, Middlesex

Printed by CS Graphics, Singapore

© Capital Transport Publishing 2000

Fifth edition

All photographs are © Capital Transport Publishing
except those supplied by the following:

Ian Bell 24, 43 top, 45 top, 56 bottom, 66 bottom, 71, 73
Hayes Davidson 72
MacCormac Jamieson Pritchard 77
London Transport Museum 7 bottom left, 9 top, 12 top, 13 top
Brian Morrison 67
Kem Rennie 32 top
David Rowe 32 bottom, 33

Preface

The London Underground is one of the world's best known transport systems. It is used extensively by Londoners and all who visit London. The diagrammatic map, the bar and circle symbol and the distinctive trains and stations are uniquely associated with the capital's metropolitan rail system. Even so, many of the Underground's lifelong users have little idea of what goes on to make it work, how its equipment operates or the historical background to the world's first urban railway. This book is a short guide around the system and gives answers to many of the questions often asked about London's Underground.

Contents

Introduction

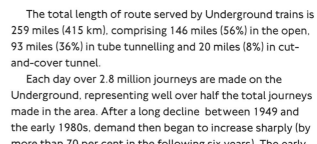

Greater London is home to over 7 million people of rich cultural diversity, occupying some 618 square miles. As Europe's leading financial services provider, it is a source of wealth to the entire nation, and has itself an economy greater than that of Hong Kong, or Austria, or Greece. London's buoyant economy attracts a vast workforce from within its own boundaries, and from a surprisingly large catchment area extending well over one hundred miles in most directions. Some 10 per cent of London's surface area is given over to highways, compared with about 25 per cent of a typical North American city, making it particularly dependent on railways for moving about.

The total length of route served by Underground trains is 259 miles (415 km), comprising 146 miles (56%) in the open, 93 miles (36%) in tube tunnelling and 20 miles (8%) in cut-and-cover tunnel.

Each day over 2.8 million journeys are made on the Underground, representing well over half the total journeys made in the area. After a long decline between 1949 and the early 1980s, demand then began to increase sharply (by more than 70 per cent in the following six years). The early 1990s brought a shallow reduction in work-related traffic because of economic recession, but recovery followed and the last years of the 1990s each broke existing records as the busiest years ever on the Underground, with 866 million journeys made in 1998/99. Culturally London had changed, with growth in retailing and leisure activity causing much of the increased travel demand at times of the day and week traditionally regarded as 'off-peak'. Rapid improvements in technology and comfort in homes, road transport and the workplace had also raised customer expectations of the travelling environment.

Through the 1990s the Underground made enormous progress in meeting these demands. In the wake of the fire at King's Cross station in 1987, safety had become the subject of systematic management techniques; the focus then turned to issues of quality and efficiency. The result was that between 1990 and 1998, in addition to carrying much increased numbers, the system also reduced accidents of all kinds, substantially increased customer satisfaction and increased its 'operating surplus' from zero to £280 million per year, this money contributing over 40 per cent of the investment in renewals and improvements.

Reliance on Government funding was, however, a major problem. Cash availability for investment was not only restricted as the rising cost of healthcare and education drained public resources, but was variable at short notice - making it increasingly difficult to plan for major infrastructure renewal – and tied to each individual fiscal year, leading to waste and a focus on short term work. The combined effect of these circumstances had meant that

only in two or three years since the 1950s had enough been spent to adequately replace worn out equipment. It was clear that the improving performance of the system could not be sustained unless this problem was tackled.

To support publicly owned enterprise, an alternative source of funding was developed in the form of the 'Private Finance Initiative', which allowed private sector investment, and which the Underground was quick to exploit. The first scheme was for the supply of a computer service at the Canary Wharf offices, but the next was much more significant, providing a new fleet of trains to the Northern line, which could not be afforded by normal funding. Others to follow were for power supplies, a new communications system and for the extension of the Piccadilly line to the proposed Terminal 5 at Heathrow Airport.

In 1998 the new Government announced its intention to extend this principle to all the system's assets, by inviting bids for the network's engineering from the private sector, in an initiative known as 'Private-Public Partnership' (PPP). Under this plan the operation of the lines would be retained in public ownership, but responsibility transferred from central government to the proposed Greater London Authority.

In preparation for this change, during 1999 the Underground changed its structural organisation from one focused on line business units, each responsible for its own operation and maintenance, to that of the new operating undertaking supported by three new 'infrastructure companies'. Each of these three would be responsible for asset supply to a group of lines:

⬩ Subsurface (District, Metropolitan, Circle, Hammersmith & City and East London);
⬩ Bakerloo, Central, Victoria and Waterloo & City;
⬩ Jubilee, Northern and Piccadilly.

In June 1999 the government announced that discussions had taken place with Railtrack in respect of the subsurface lines, following proposals from that organisation to provide through running between the National rail network and the Underground, over the East London line and the north side of the Circle line, the Circle later being ruled out as having insufficient capacity. Bids for asset supply to all three groups were subsequently opened up to all suitable parties and there was also some campaigning for other forms of financing as the 20th century drew to a close, including a bond issue.

What everyone is in agreement with is that the new arrangements for injecting new money into the Underground will need to meet the increasing needs of London over the first three decades of the new century, and ensure that this vital support to the region's economy can be sustained.

 # History

Below Farringdon station (originally called Farringdon Street) was the eastern extremity of the Metropolitan Railway's original line which opened on 10 January 1863. Some elements of the original station are still present.

The first underground railway in the world started operating when the Metropolitan Railway opened a line between Bishops Road, Paddington and Farringdon on 10th January 1863. At the Paddington end there was a connection to the Great Western Railway and, during the first few months of operation, the Great Western loaned locomotives and rolling stock to the Metropolitan. After one of the disputes which characterised the relationship between the two companies for many years, the Great Western withdrew its rolling stock and the Metropolitan prevailed upon the Great Northern Railway company to help it out until stock of its own could be built. By July 1864 the Metropolitan had enough of its own stock to operate the service without assistance.

Specially designed steam locomotives were purchased by the Metropolitan for working in their tunnels. They were built by Beyer Peacock of Manchester and were fitted with a system for condensing the exhaust steam to reduce the smoke appearing in the tunnels. The locomotives were of the 4-4-0 tank engine type and they became the standard for both the Metropolitan and District Railways. An example of one of them has survived to be preserved in the London Transport Museum, Covent Garden.

After the opening of the initial section in 1863, there were various extensions to the east and the line reached Aldgate in 1876. It was further extended round to a station called Tower of London (on the site of the present Tower Hill) in 1882. A westward projection was started from a

Left Although the steam locomotives employed by the Metropolitan and District railways were designed to consume their own smoke by diverting it into the engine's water tanks, in practice they needed to be able to expel it as frequently as possible. Therefore ventilation shafts were built from the tunnel roofs to the outside, usually into the squares or gardens above. This ventilation aperture remains at Great Portland Street station.

Below left Steam locomotive No. 55 pulling a train to Hammersmith shortly before being replaced by electric trains in 1905. Engine No. 23 of similar appearance is preserved at the LT Museum.

Below right Map produced by the Metropolitan Railway in 1882 showing the Inner Circle line complete in all but the section between Liverpool Street and Tower Hill. Parliament had to intervene to compel the Met and District railways to complete the link.

junction at Praed Street between the stations at Paddington and Edgware Road. This line passed through a new Paddington station built exclusively for the Metropolitan (the present Circle/District line station), proceeded south to High Street Kensington and then curved east to South Kensington, which was reached in 1868.

At this point a second underground railway company entered the story. This was the Metropolitan District Railway, usually referred to as the District. The District built the southern section of the present-day Circle line between South Kensington and Mansion House, opening it in stages between 1868 and 1871. The present Embankment along the north shore of the Thames was built during this period as part of the construction of the District's tunnels between Westminster and Temple.

The final part of the Circle was opened in 1884 when the joint construction by the Metropolitan and District of the link between Mansion House and the Tower was completed.

The project included an extension to Whitechapel and a triangular junction with the present-day Circle line between Liverpool Street, Aldgate East and the Tower.

Both the District and Metropolitan became involved in the construction or operation of extensions radiating from the Circle line. Jointly with the Great Western, the Metropolitan operated a branch to Hammersmith which was opened in 1864. This line, like the first section of the Circle to Farringdon, was constructed to take the Great Western's broad gauge rolling stock. The track was laid as mixed gauge to allow both 4ft 8½in and 7ft 0½in gauge rolling stock to operate. Traces of this can still be seen today in the wide gaps between tracks on the Hammersmith branch and the generous tunnel clearances between Paddington and Farringdon.

The District reached Hammersmith in 1874 and then built a further short extension to a junction with the London & South Western Railway at Studland Road near what is now Ravenscourt Park station. This gave the District access to Richmond to which point it began running trains in 1877.

In 1879 it opened an extension from Turnham Green to Ealing Broadway.

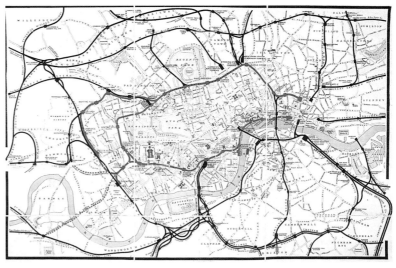

Right The Metropolitan Railway's lines running through north west London, Middlesex, Hertfordshire and Buckinghamshire followed the practice of other main line railways. This called for signalling systems designed to handle freight as well as passenger trains. A few signal boxes still exist, as does this one at Chesham.

Below Kennington was built as one of the City & South London stations, but was greatly expanded when the Charing Cross, Euston & Hampstead Railway was extended to form a junction with the original line in 1926.

In the following year the branch to West Brompton (opened 1869) was extended to Putney Bridge and, following the construction of a bridge across the river to connect with the London & South Western Railway at East Putney, District trains were allowed running powers to Wimbledon in 1889.

During this period the Metropolitan was also expanding. Apart from the line to Hammersmith already mentioned, a branch from Baker Street to Swiss Cottage was opened in 1868. This was extended to Willesden Green in 1879 and to Harrow-on-the-Hill in 1880. Pinner was reached in 1885, Rickmansworth in 1887 and Chesham in 1889.

All the services on the Metropolitan and District Railways were originally steam operated, the District using the same 4-4-0 condensing tank locomotives as the Metropolitan. The District had 4-wheeled wooden carriages, usually formed into 9-coach sets for its trains. The Metropolitan also had some 4-wheeled stock but the bulk of its trains had

8-wheeled coaches, the four axles being on a rigid wheelbase. Bogie stock did not appear until 1898. However, by this time, a new form of motive power had come to the Underground for in 1890 electric traction was introduced with the opening of the City & South London Railway.

The City & South London Railway was officially opened on 4th November 1890 by the then Prince of Wales, later King Edward VII, between Stockwell and King William Street in the City of London. It was the first tube railway in the

Right Interior of an 1890 car built for the City & South London service between the City and Clapham. Since the trains ran entirely within tunnels with guards at the ends of each car, announcing the names of stations, it was assumed that passengers would not need to see out. However, in an endeavour to get away from the claustrophobic atmosphere of what passengers had called padded cells, later cars were built with normal depth windows.

world and the first underground railway to be operated by electricity. Although it was the pioneer of electric traction in London, the C&SLR almost missed this distinction. When work on the tunnelling of the line was started, it was envisaged that the system of traction would be cable haulage. It was to have been based on the system introduced in San Francisco for the now world-famous cable cars. By the time the C&SLR was opened however, electric traction had been substituted as its traction system, and the company led the way for London's future rapid transit systems. In 1898 the short tube line between Waterloo and the City was opened by the London & South Western Railway and the Metropolitan and District Railways began conversion to electric traction in the early 1900s.

The C&SLR was opened with dc electric locomotives hauling trains consisting of three small carriages. The locomotives were only fourteen feet long. The carriages were specially designed to fit in the 10ft 2in diameter of the original tunnels. They were 27 feet long and weighed only 7 tons. Since they were to run only in tunnels, it was thought that they did not need full-size windows, so only small glazed panels were fitted to the bodysides just below gutter level. There were no other windows. Inside, there were longitudinal benches fitted with buttoned upholstery up to the base of the glazed panels. Entrances for the cars were provided at the ends, where double sliding doors gave access to open platforms. The platforms had gates which were closed between stations and opened by 'gatemen' to allow passengers to board and alight. The lack of proper windows meant that the gatemen had to announce the stations to the passengers and the noise level was such that the names had to be shouted if people were to hear them.

In 1900 the C&SLR opened extensions to Clapham Common in the south and to Moorgate in the north. The Moorgate extension allowed the original terminus at King William Street to be abandoned, being replaced by a station at Bank. A further extension of the line to Angel was opened in 1901 and another to Euston was opened in 1907.

In spite of its primitive technology, the C&SLR, which is now part of the Northern (via Bank) line, was regarded as a success and it encouraged the building of other tube lines. In 1900 the Central London Railway was opened between Shepherd's Bush and Bank, cutting right across the central area within the Circle line and connecting the shopping district of Oxford Street with the financial district in the City. It also provided access to the then fashionable suburb of Shepherd's Bush. Like the C&SLR, this line opened with electric locomotives hauling passenger cars, but the trains were up to seven cars long. However, after only three years of operation the locomotives were replaced because of their excessive vibration. Multiple-unit traction then became the standard

system of operation. This provided drivers' cabs at each end of each train and eliminated locomotive changing at termini. With a service frequency of up to 30 trains per hour, the Central London Railway became London's first tube rapid transit railway.

More tube lines appeared following the opening of the Central London. The Bakerloo, Piccadilly and Hampstead lines were all opened during 1906-7. They formed the cores of the much longer lines now seen today. The Bakerloo was the first of the three to open, on 10th March 1906. It was originally known as the Baker Street and Waterloo Railway, although it originally ran from Baker Street to the station now known as Lambeth North and was extended to Elephant & Castle in August 1906. Extensions of the line to the north west were opened in stages over the next ten years, reaching Edgware Road in June 1907, Queen's Park and Willesden Junction in 1915 and Watford in 1917. Between Queen's Park and Watford the Bakerloo trains ran over the new tracks specially constructed by the London & North Western Railway next to its main line for its own suburban electric service. At that time the Bakerloo was the longest of the tube lines and remained so until the opening of the Piccadilly extensions in 1932-33.

The Piccadilly line was opened as the Great Northern, Piccadilly and Brompton Railway in December 1906. It ran between Finsbury Park and Hammersmith and had a small branch from the main route at Holborn to Aldwych opened in November 1907.

The Hampstead line was the last of the lines to be opened as a result of the tube railway boom of the 1900s. It opened between Charing Cross and Golders Green (with a branch to Highgate) in 1907 and eventually became part of the Northern line after being combined with the rebuilt C&SLR.

By the time they were opened, the Bakerloo, Piccadilly and Hampstead lines were all owned by Yerkes' holding company which was known as the Underground Electric Railways of London Ltd (UERL) which by now had also taken over the District Railway. The three tubes were formed into a common company called the London Electric Railway (LER). The UERL also absorbed the Central London and the C&SLR in 1913.

The three Yerkes tubes began their operations with multiple unit trains. As on the older tubes, the cars had open end entrances with iron lattice or grille gates. The first Metropolitan and District electric stock also had open ends but they quickly introduced enclosed entrances and middle doors to both improve weather protection and speed up station stops. The tube lines began introducing these improvements from 1915 and, from the early 1920s, they introduced air operated sliding doors on all new tube cars.

Both the Central London and the C&SLR had slightly smaller tunnels than the three LER tubes. A start was made towards standardisation during the 1920s when the C&SLR was enlarged to match the LER tunnel size and was extended south to Morden. The improvements to the C&SLR were designed to combine the line with the Hampstead. The two lines were connected at Kennington and Camden Town and the Hampstead line was extended from Golders Green to Edgware.

Right Mosaic Underground symbol which can still be seen at Maida Vale.

Far right Tiled ticket office window surround. Most surfaces were tiled to make cleaning easier.

The Central London Railway was extended from Bank to Liverpool Street in 1912 and to Ealing Broadway in 1920 over a line built in a partnership with the Great Western Railway, but it had to wait until 1938 for its tunnels to be enlarged to normal tube size. This was done as part of the plans for long eastern and western extensions to Epping, Hainault, Ongar and West Ruislip. The second world war delayed these but they were opened soon after.

The idea of extending the tube lines to create suburbs and thus generate custom had begun in 1907 with the opening of the Hampstead tube to the open countryside at Golders Green. It was thought, rightly, that residential development would occur if good transport was provided. The idea had been imported from the United States with Yerkes and his engineers, who had seen the same phenomenon in cities like New York and Chicago.

The Piccadilly line was perhaps the classic example of the Underground Company's ideal of a tube line extended to serve the new suburbs, thus tapping new demand to fill the under-utilised tunnels through the central area. This line was substantially extended in the early 1930s to the west over two District line branches, whilst breaking new ground to the north with an extension part in tunnel and part on (or above) the surface.

The extension to Oakwood was the last under independent ownership; four months later the modest further extension to Cockfosters was the first to open under the auspices of the new London Passenger Transport Board, on 31st July 1933.

In 1933 the London Passenger Transport Board was appointed by the national government to take over the operation of the Underground railways and bus and tram services in what is now the greater London area. The name London Transport appeared for the first time on buses and trains to mark the passing of the Underground and bus companies from private to public ownership. The LPTB immediately began a programme of new works which included a new tube line between Baker Street and Finchley Road to relieve the Metropolitan's worst bottleneck, the extension of the Northern north of Highgate and the Central line extensions already mentioned. Much new rolling stock was acquired, including the 1938 tube stock which was

In the 1920s Tube lines were extended to fill the gaps not served by the main line railways. Stations at first followed traditional architectural practice, as at Hendon Central on the Hampstead tube, seen with a train of Standard stock.

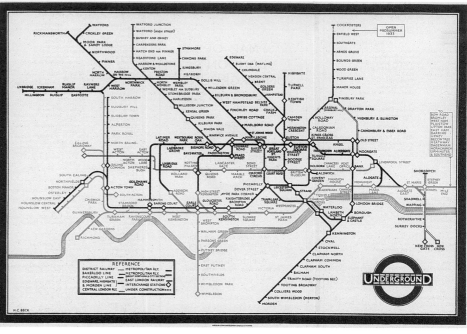

Once built, the Underground needed to constantly remind people of its existence and convenience, especially outside the rush hours when trains were running empty. The Underground's bullseye appeared on book matches as well as the more familiar map, redrawn by Henry Beck in diagrammatic form to make the system easier to understand.

withdrawn from the Underground in 1988 and some of which is now in use on the Isle of Wight.

Following the second world war there was a change of government and virtually all the railways in Britain were nationalised in 1948. London Transport remained much the same as before as far as the public was concerned. A bigger change occurred in 1970 when political control passed to the Greater London Council. Control reverted to the government from June 1984 when London Regional Transport was set up. London Underground Ltd was formed as a subsidiary of LRT on 1st April 1985.

The Victoria line, the first Underground line to be fully equipped for automatic train operation (ATO) was opened in stages between 1968 and 1971. Another new line — the Jubilee line — was formed from the Stanmore branch of the Bakerloo and a new tube built between Baker Street and Charing Cross. It opened in 1979. After many false starts, work commenced late in 1993 on an important extension to serve London's former Docklands.

In 1977 the Piccadilly line extension

to Heathrow Airport was opened. The building of a new terminal (Terminal 4) later became necessary and it was decided to include a link for the Underground. A single-track loop extension to the Piccadilly line was constructed and it opened in 1986.

The London Underground has also had a distinguished history in the development of its public image and the approach to art. The best known symbol of the Underground is the bar and circle. About 1908, a version of the now familiar symbol, which had a solid red disc, appeared on station platforms as a way of displaying the station name. Shortly after the bar and disc device started to appear, a new corporate typeface was introduced on the Underground. It was designed by Edward Johnston and was used on new signs and publicity from 1916. It has remained in use with only minor modification to this day — as clear and crisp as ever — a tribute to the simplicity and clarity of the original design. Johnston also redesigned the bar and disc symbol so that it became the bar and circle device similar to that used today. During the expansion of the system in the 1920s and 1930s it was incorporated into exterior designs and is now universally used to say 'Here is the Underground'.

Right Events that could be reached by Underground were advertised within the cars. It was on the design of these small posters that many designers later to be famous cut their teeth.

Below To match the new aesthetic impetus, the bullseye design was also refined.

Below right Good design remains a feature of Underground publicity today.

The London Underground has become renowned throughout the world as a leader in the use of high quality art in its publicity. Posters displayed on stations have been prominent in the use of works by artists specially commissioned by the Underground. The famous Underground line diagram has become an internationally acknowledged masterpiece and its principles have been adopted by transport organisations throughout the world. It was originally designed by Henry Beck in 1931 and published two years later. The poster tradition continued throughout the 1920s and 1930s with work by such artists as Graham Sutherland, E. McKnight Kauffer and many others. The posters became so popular that they have been reproduced for sale to the public as well as revived for publicity purposes. Today the tradition continues as posters specially commissioned by the Underground continue to appear on stations advertising events and locations which can be reached by Underground.

ZOO NIGHTS

TO 11 P.M. ON WEDNESDAYS AND THURSDAYS UNTIL AUGUST 31

STATIONS: CAMDEN TOWN, CHALK FARM OR LORDS

Simply Summer

Get up and go with your guide to Summer in the city

Making London simple

Simply Fashion

Get into the capital's fashion scene by Tube and bus

Making London simple

Stations are regarded as one of the most important parts of the London Underground infrastructure. As a shopkeeper will provide an attractive window display to entice customers inside to buy his goods, so the Underground must provide attractive stations to persuade customers to sample its services. The diverse origins of many of the lines forming the Underground have left a legacy of variety in station design in addition to the range of site needs ranging from deep-level tube lines in the centre of the city to stations serving small country towns in the outer suburbs.

The street access to every station is marked by the world-famous Underground logo. Before this came into use stations had used the traditional British form of displaying the name of the company and station on the exterior of the street level building and the name of the station at each end of the platforms. The tube lines incorporated the station name in the tiling of platform walls together with 'Way Out' signs. The bar and disc signs appeared on platforms from about 1908 and in 1937 a frieze was added repeating the station name along the length of the platform.

None of the initial station buildings opened with the first underground railway on the north side of the Circle line between Paddington and Farringdon is still to be seen today in original condition. However, a good idea of what they were like can be seen at Bayswater, where the original building of 1868 is still in use and still in some respects as built. All of the stations on the sub-surface lines are close enough to the surface to allow access to the platforms by stairs.

Many of the Circle stations were built in an open cutting and originally provided with an arched overall roof. One of the best remaining examples can be seen at Paddington, where the platforms have been restored to near their

original condition. The air space over stations like this can become a lucrative asset if developed as a property site. Early examples were the flats over Baker Street station known as Chiltern Court, which were completed in 1929, and London Underground's own headquarters at St James's Park which were opened the same year. In recent times more commercial development has taken place at a number of sites including large projects at Barbican, Mansion House and Gloucester Road. The site of the District and Piccadilly lines station at Hammersmith has been developed into a major shopping and office centre.

When an extra pair of tracks was built in 1866 between King's Cross and Moorgate to cope with main line rail traffic wishing to use the Metropolitan's route, the stations had to be enlarged. Farringdon and Barbican (then Aldersgate) are still much as they were then and Farringdon still sports its

Facing page top The four platforms at the District line's spacious Earl's Court are covered by a high overall roof dating from 1878.

Facing page bottom Croxley and Watford were built in this style by the Metropolitan Railway for its new branch line opened in 1925. A similar style was adopted for stations on the Stanmore branch, opened in 1932.

Right Clapham South was the first station to be opened on the City & South London Railway's extension from Clapham Common to Morden in 1926. All were built to the designs of the architect Charles Holden.

Below North Ealing was built on the District Railway's branch from Ealing Common to South Harrow and opened in 1903. District trains were replaced by those of the Piccadilly line in 1932.

magnificent twin overall roof. Another station with a fine overall roof is Earl's Court. The roof dates from 1878, whilst the Earl's Court Road entrance was rebuilt in 1906 by the District's architect Harry Ford in the style similar to that of Leslie Green for the three LER tubes which were being completed at that time.

As lines were extended into the suburbs and the open air, so stations developed in a similar style to those of other railways. The buildings at Rickmansworth are typical of the 1880s expansion period on the Metropolitan, whilst the later suburban style of the 1920s can be seen at Croxley. The country flavour is much more apparent here, especially when compared with the Portland stone faced frontages of Charles Holden for the tube lines of that era (eg Clapham South to Morden).

The District also extended into the suburbs, particularly in west London, but few of the original station buildings have survived, most having been rebuilt during the 1930s. One which has is at North Ealing, which dates from 1903, where the original station house incorporated a first floor flat built for the District Inspector.

Architect Leslie Green has already been mentioned. He was responsible for the deep-red terracotta tiled station

Left The original facade of the Great Northern Piccadilly & Brompton Railway's Gloucester Road station was built to the designs of Leslie Green and opened in 1906. Many of these terracotta facades still survive, including some which are no longer in use as station entrances.

Below Completed in 1928, Burnt Oak was built to the designs of Stanley Heaps.

Top right Regarded as one of the finest examples of the architect Charles Holden, Southgate was opened in 1933. The building survives in almost the same state as it was opened, together with the vintage road sign post outside.

Middle right Opposite the exhibition site this Warwick Road entrance, which was built in 1937, serves Earl's Court station. The upper floor was added in 1965 to house the Control Room for the District and Piccadilly lines.

frontages of the tube expansions between 1906 and the First World War. Excellent examples of these include Mornington Crescent, Russell Square and Gloucester Road.

The expansion of the tube lines in the 1920s and 1930s created a new era for station design in London. Such was the quality of the designs introduced during this period that many of the buildings are now 'listed' and cannot be altered without good cause. The Portland stone buildings of the southern end of the Northern line have already been mentioned and further examples of Holden's first Underground style are to be seen at Hounslow West and Ealing Common. Another 1920s station entrance style, with elements of the Georgian and Roman, by the Underground's

own architect, Stanley A. Heaps, can be seen north of Golders Green, Brent Cross and Burnt Oak being excellent examples.

The early 1930s produced the fine brickwork surface structures seen along the western and northern ends of the Piccadilly line. Southgate, Arnos Grove, Northfields, Oakwood, Sudbury Hill and Sudbury Town all show the large round or rectangular surface buildings typical of this time.

Below Charles Holden's Arnos Grove of 1932.

Above The rebuilt Rayners Lane station was opened in 1938. The high-ceilinged booking hall is a feature of many of the Piccadilly line suburban stations.

Left The present station at Northfields was opened in 1932 on the Hounslow branch of the District Railway. Piccadilly line trains shared the line from 1933 until 1964 when they took sole possession.

Bottom left The dramatic bus station at the forecourt of Newbury Park station was opened in 1949 when Underground services started running to Hainault.

The Central line extensions mark the next big stage in the architectural development of the Underground. Opened in the 1940s, various modern designs appeared, notably at Hanger Lane, Loughton, Wanstead, Redbridge and Gants Hill. Many of the stations at the eastern end of the Central were taken over from the LNER at that time and date from the late nineteenth century.

Blackhorse Road, the only new surface building on the Victoria line when it opened, offers a fine example of 1960s thinking, as do Surrey Quays and Shadwell for the 1970s. A startlingly refreshing new station was built at Hillingdon in the early 1990s as a result of the A40 road construction which obliterated the site of its predecessor: this was the first to have specific lift provision for the mobility-impaired from the outset.

All ticket halls were affected by the 'Underground Ticketing System' implemented in the 1980s, with new

ticket offices and, at central locations, automatic gates as well. Gates were installed at small numbers of additional stations through the 1990s until a final push for their universal provision started in late 1998 under the 'Prestige' Private Finance Initiative.

Fire safety precautions have also had an impact on appearances, often to provide detection and alarm systems, and always to remove melamines and other materials having unsatisfactory fire performance. Similarly, the need for security and monitoring equipment has impinged on stations. Given the large number of sites of special architectural importance on the Underground, these programmes have had to be progressed sensitively, but the result has usually been one of excellent restoration.

Left Stratford station was transformed for the coming of the Jubilee line, the architecture forming a gateway to the tantalising 'Docklands experience' beyond.

Below Not an airport terminal, but the ticket hall at the west end of Canary Wharf. The new stations on this line bear little resemblance to their forebears. They make a bold statement to the prospective customer, yet most have simple and functional finishes. They have dual access for safety and to widen their catchment and, above all, space – space to move, to give flexibility and to allow for the future.

Right The dramatic entrance to Canary Wharf station, opened in September 1999. A bank of escalators leads down to the large ticket hall.

Trains

All London Underground passenger trains are powered by dc electricity at a nominal 630 volts, using an unusual four-rail system (with an insulated negative return rail in the centre of the track). Most fleets have both power and trailer cars, although some have only power cars. There are also works locomotives which can be powered by batteries, and a few using diesel engines.

All trains use compressed air for brakes, door operation and other ancillary equipment, while lighting and electrical control circuits operate at various voltages, generated locally on each train.

The trains' air brakes were originally controlled by a solely pneumatic system, but this was inherently unsuitable for intensive stop-start operations, and from the mid 1930s electric control was used for normal service braking, with pneumatic control retained for the fail-safe emergency brake. The 1973, 'D' and all subsequent stocks have a fail-safe form of electrical control for the air brake, and the pneumatic control, present from the very earliest passenger trains, was omitted for the first time.

Trains built from the mid 1960s onwards use regenerative braking to supplement the air-applied friction brakes, thus reducing the consumption of brake blocks and, importantly, generation of dust. Because of the unrefined nature of the power supply, the current generated by electrical braking has to be wasted as heat by resistors under the train on most stocks, However, from the 1992 stock trains have been capable of feeding the current back into the track, and the Central line was the first to benefit when the line's power feeding arrangements were upgraded in the mid 1990s.

The shape and size of the trains is dictated by the size of tunnels and station platform lengths. There are two basic types – subsurface and tube (this latter title is widely used to describe the Underground generally, although strictly it does not apply to all lines). The subsurface trains are similar in size to 'main line' trains in Britain, and are restricted to the lines around the Circle, whose tunnels were constructed by cut and cover methods, housing two tracks. These were generally the first sections to be built: most later lines (from 1890 onwards) were bored through the ground to avoid surface disruption, to a small diameter and accommodating only a single track in each bore. Tube trains are therefore significantly smaller.

Because of operation in tunnel, the trains have always used the latest techniques to ensure easy evacuation in emergency, and high standards of fire safety. The trains usually last for around 35 to 40 years, and improvements in fire technology have led to all but the newest trains undergoing refurbishment, with new interiors and in some cases new wiring too. The opportunity was also taken to provide better communications and information systems and, in trains with more than a few years' residual life, to provide a new interior layout and radically improved finish. The exteriors were painted in a new livery, obliterating the aluminium which had become weathered and pitted, and resisting graffiti much more effectively. So successful was this process that the majority of passengers believed refurbished trains to be new, rather than having typically twenty years' service behind them.

One person operation was introduced with automatic trains on the Victoria line when it opened in 1968, and then spread to most other lines by converting existing trains through the 1980s. On the Central and Northern lines the trains had too little life left to justify the high costs of conversion, and guards remained on these lines until 1995 and 2000 respectively, as new trains were commissioned.

Guards had, on most stocks, operated from the gangway at the leading end of the last car (the gangway being available as a normal doorway for passengers when elsewhere in the formation). Conversion to one person operation involved moving the door, heating and lighting controls to the driving cab. Conversion of trains on tube lines also included the provision of a radio alarm system to alert the Line Controller to a driver becoming incapacitated. Stations served by one-person trains were also provided with mirrors and closed circuit television to enable the Operator to control the doors safely, but on the Central, Northern and Jubilee lines this has now been superseded by the new trains having in-cab television. It is intended to extend this practice to all lines, although the restricted size of cabs on the older stocks offers something of a challenge to the designers.

Tube lines

The 1967 and 1972 stocks

When the Victoria line was opened in 1968, it was equipped from the outset with automatically driven trains, known as 1967 stock. These trains had wraparound windscreens and panoramic side windows, and thus looked much more modern than anything seen on the Underground before. Technically there were some advances too, but in many respects they represented an evolutionary – rather than revolutionary – step forward from earlier trains. Internally the trains used plastics quite extensively, rather than the varnished wood and painted finishes Londoners were used to, and although the effect was very 'modern' at the time, the unrelieved greys soon became tired and somewhat dated.

By the beginning of the 1970s, it had been decided to extend the Piccadilly line to Heathrow Airport, and it was recognised that trains with more luggage provision would be needed there. The plan was to buy new trains for the Piccadilly and cascade the 1959 stock from there to the Northern. To make up the shortfall of the total Northern line fleet, thirty trains of 1972 stock were produced, representing just under one third of its stock. These looked very much the same as the 1967 stock, but had seven rather than eight cars, and were provided with equipment for two-person operation. A second batch followed in 1973, comprising 33 trains; these had certain modifications and were designated 1972 MkII. The intention was that the MkII stock would initially enter service on the Northern line, pending the arrival of the 1959 stock from the Piccadilly, and thus allow early withdrawal of the increasingly troublesome 1938 stock then operating the Northern. The MkIIs would then transfer to the recently authorised Fleet line, actually opened as the Jubilee.

In practice, the Jubilee line works ran late, as did the delivery of new trains for the Piccadilly, and these trains spent longer on the Northern than intended. They did eventually provide the initial service on the Jubilee, when it opened in 1979, but were later displaced to the Bakerloo, where they operate today. The first batch of 1972s (which became known as 1972 MkI) became depleted over the years as some were converted to 1967 specification to increase the Victoria line fleet, and others transferred to the Bakerloo. By 1996 only 20 of the original 30 were left on the Northern, and these were all withdrawn in November 1998 with the advent of new trains there, some being placed in store for further use elsewhere.

In 1989, refurbishment work started on these trains, with grabrails, seating and flooring colour-coded to the line identity. In practice, only three of the Northern line trains were treated, and these were refitted to transfer to the Bakerloo after running on the Northern for a brief period.

The 1973 and 1983 stocks

With the decision to extend the Piccadilly line to Heathrow Airport, it was appreciated that more trains would be needed, and that additional luggage space was required. It was therefore decided to order a fleet of new trains, which received the designation 1973 stock.

These were the first to have all-electric control of the air brakes, and the first to have six long cars in the formation, rather than seven standard length vehicles. This provided a train about 6 metres shorter than those they replaced, at lower cost but with very similar capacity. Disadvantages included the need for a slightly narrower carbody to cope with twisting tunnels, and larger platform gaps at curved platforms. Luggage accommodation was provided by having more 'stand back' space at the doorways. The trains entered service between 1975 and 1978.

In 1990, with refurbishment of the 1967/72 stocks under way, one unit of 1973 stock received a pilot refurbishment, based on the earlier work but representing a considerable further design advance. In particular, car end windows were provided for added passenger security, and the centre bays of each car were provided with luggage racks and a variety of novel seating layouts. Many lessons were learned from this prototype, and the production version adopted all-longitudinal seating, with the desired increased luggage accommodation achieved by further extending the 'standback' areas by the doorways. This provision proved very beneficial in clearing crowds on the line's busy central section, and gave just enough space to accommodate a standard wheelchair. Lighting was arranged in a pair of continuous strips, and the overall appearance 'cleaned up' when compared with earlier refurbishments. The first refurbished train entered service in 1996, with the programme scheduled to finish in 2000.

The 1983 stock, dimensionally similar to the 1973 stock but designed with single-leaf doors, was replaced on the Jubilee in 1998. No home could be found for the first batch, which required considerable expenditure to overcome design defects, and most cars were scrapped. The Mark II batch was placed into storage for refurbishment and conversion for use on the Piccadilly line, to enable frequencies to be increased. The work includes rebuilding the cars with conventional double-leaf doors at the inboard position: the single-leaf doors would not adequately cope with platform loadings on this busy line. The trains are due to enter service on the Piccadilly during 2001.

1992 – a new structural solution

By the early 1980s, rolling stock technology was developing on a number of fronts, and this culminated in the purchase of 1986 experimental stock, intended as a test bed for a new generation of trains for the Central line. Three versions of the stock were produced, each comprising two units of two cars, thus producing two six-car trains. All cars were of monocoque construction, rather than the heavy solebar with lightweight superstructure concept used on all previous Underground trains, and for the first time the sliding doors were externally hung rather than opening into pockets within the body structure. Electronic control of the dc traction motors was used, offering lower energy consumption and smoother acceleration than the electro-mechanical control used on all other Underground trains.

The experience gained was used for the specification of the 1992 stock for the Central line, which totalled 85 trains. Because of tight curves on the line, the longer carbodies used for 1973 and 1983 stocks could not be employed, and these trains have eight cars of conventional length. The passenger doors are wider than used previously, and like the refurbished 1973 stock, all seats are longitudinal. During the development of the design, British Rail decided to replace the 1940 vintage cars on the Waterloo & City line, and a further five 4-car trains were ordered for onward delivery to that organisation as its Class 482. The cars were identical to those on the Central apart from the external livery, which was to Network SouthEast standard. Ironically, with the privatisation of British Rail the line passed into London Underground ownership in 1994 and has since been operated as part of the Central line. There is no physical connection between the Waterloo & City and any other railway, however, and the trains have not been mixed.

The new trains entered service between 1993 and 1995, and introduced one-person operation to the Central line. They were fitted for automatic operation, but because of ongoing problems with the new signalling system, introduction of the feature was delayed for some years. In the meantime the trains became the first on the Underground to be driven manually with Automatic Train Protection rather than mechanical tripcocks.

1995 and 1996 stocks

Somewhat oddly, the 1996 stock (Jubilee line) was ordered before the 1995 trains (Northern), and has technologically less advanced equipment.

The design was originated in about 1991 for the Jubilee line extension, and it was intended to buy new cars to mix with the existing 1983 stock to produce hybrid trains. The new cars were to feature the stronger structure and externally hung doors of the 1992 stock, but were of more conventional appearance to match the older cars. This design was retained when it was decided to provide a wholly new fleet, and 59 trains of 1996 stock were delivered from 1996 onwards. Most of the trains were delivered to the Jubilee depot at Neasden, but some were sent by road to the new depot at Stratford Market to initiate trials at the east end of the new line. The first of the new trains entered service in December 1997; within a few months all of the 1983 stock had been displaced. Each car is of similar length to 1973 and 1983 stock, and trains similarly consist of six cars. As demand rises on the Jubilee, however, there is provision to add a further car, and all platforms on the line are already sufficiently long.

For many years plans had been under development for the modernisation of the Northern line, and a number of possible rolling stock designs were submitted by leading design houses as early as 1992. Some novel features were proposed, including full width gangways between cars. All featured smaller wheels than used hitherto, enabling them to fit entirely below floor level and thus allowing doors to be located anywhere along the carbody. Regrettably, falling income from government thwarted the scheme, and no further progress was made.

In 1994 the Government announced its Private Finance Initiative, paving the way for public sector undertakings to benefit from private investment, and work started on procuring a new fleet of trains for the Northern by this means. In due course a contract was signed with GEC Alsthom for the supply of serviceable trains on a daily basis, which resulted in the supply of the 1995 stock, the first of which entered service in June 1998, providing a great improvement in travelling environment for customers and staff. The trains, which are owned by the suppliers and their financiers, not by the Underground, were developed from the 1996 stock, but using new technology where this had developed since the 1996 design was 'frozen' in 1991. Outwardly the two fleets are almost identical.

Sub-surface trains

'A' Stock for Amersham

This stock was devised during the late 1950s to replace a variety of slam-door multiple unit and locomotive hauled carriages on the Metropolitan 'main' line between the City, Baker Street and the affluent Buckinghamshire hills, at the time of electrification of the line north of Rickmansworth. Two batches were built and entered service between 1961 and 1963. The first, designated 'A60' was to provide the fleet for the Amersham and Chesham services; the second (A62) to displace sliding-door trains from the Uxbridge and Watford services to the District, and enable the withdrawal of some antique trains there.

The trains are formed into four-car units, and operate as such on the East London line and Chesham shuttle service. On the Metropolitan 'main line', they now operate only as eight-car trains, the practice of uncoupling units for the off-peak service having been abandoned in the 1980s.

In 1994 a process of refurbishing the cars was started. The line suffers more than most with petty vandalism, and the train interiors had become very scruffy indeed. Some debate took place before the work started, as the trains were already relatively old, and had a limited residual lifespan. As they had a low priority for replacement in the short term, it was thus decided to carry out a limited refurbishment, with external painting, new interior finishes and car end windows, but without the major re-equipping of the saloon that tube stocks were enjoying. The programme was completed during 1998.

'C' for the Circle

The wholly urban nature of the Circle and Hammersmith lines, coupled with the relative design freedom available on subsurface stocks, allowed the C stock to be purpose built to clear large numbers of people from busy platforms, and each car has four double doorways. This feature has proved outstandingly successful in carrying large numbers of passengers over the relatively short distances most use these lines for.

Trains were delivered in two batches. The first, C69, arrived in 1970–71 for the Circle and Hammersmith lines, the second (C77) entering service in 1978, enabling the type to be extended to the District line's Edgware Road and Wimbledon service. The two batches are virtually identical. The cars are formed into two-car units, operating in threes to make six-car trains. These are the shortest trains operating through central London, limited by the length of platforms around the west side of the Circle.

These trains became early candidates for refurbishment and this was carried out between 1991 and 1994, completely transforming the interiors.

D78 – for the District

Much-travelled pre-war stock displaced from the Circle and associated services was becoming very troublesome through the 1970s, and it became necessary to consider replacement. The District was also home to the 'R' stock, an eclectic collection of cars from various vintages, but having a fairly homogenous appearance to customers. A few of the cars had pioneered aluminium construction in 1949, and some were built as recently as 1959, but it was decided to clear all the existing trains out, and avoid the problems of small residual fleets of older trains.

The D stock was designed to operate over the whole of the District except the Wimbledon–Edgware Road section for which the cars are too long, and was technically based on the 1973 tube stock, with some lessons learned. The similarity extends to the use of tube-sized wheels for the first time, and the six 'long' car formation. The trains were provided with single-leaf doorways throughout, and the generous circulating area near the doorways avoided this feature causing the dwell time problems experienced with the 1983 tube stock.

Engineers' trains

The Underground operates a variety of vehicles for engineering purposes. The most elusive to the majority of passengers are the works trains, consisting of wagons carrying materials and equipment to maintain the track and other fixed infrastructure. These are marshalled between battery locomotives, and usually move under 'mains' power to and from the overnight worksite, but then using their own batteries once at work when traction current is switched off to the rails. They are normally based at the works depots at Lillie Bridge (near West Kensington, and the original Piccadilly line depot in 1906) and Ruislip (Central line). Sometimes they can be seen running between these depots during the day, but are mostly seen only by those waiting for the first or last passenger trains of the day.

Facing page top The tunnel cleaning train is used in tube tunnels throughout the network to remove dust which, if allowed to accumulate, could form both a fire and a health hazard. The leading car is adapted from 1938 tube stock, once the mainstay of the Bakerloo and Northern lines; beyond is one of two 'vacuum' cars, inhaling and storing the dust dislodged by powerful air jets.

Facing page bottom Another conversion from a passenger train is the weedkilling train, which forms an economical way of keeping lineside vegetation under control. Unlike the tunnel cleaning train, this one can be used at normal line speeds and work among service trains.

Below Between 1938 and 1974 many of these battery locomotives were built to a virtually identical design. They can use both mains electricity from the track and battery power, and are invariably used in pairs, marshalled at either end of the works train.

Equally rarely seen is the tunnel cleaning train, consisting of three specially constructed blower/vacuum cars which dislodge and store the accumulated dust from the tunnels. They are marshalled between former 1938 stock passenger cars provided with special motor control equipment so that they can crawl continuously at low speed through the tunnels. Also using former passenger cars, though this time painted in normal train livery rather than the yellow of works trains, is the track recording unit. This uses a former 1973 stock trailer car to monitor track condition, driven at each end by converted power cars of 1960 stock, prototypes of what had been intended to be a large fleet for the Central. This is the only engineers' train regularly used during the day.

In addition, the Underground owns and leases a variety of specialist railborne equipment to maintain and condition the track and other structures.

Bakerloo line

Elephant & Castle to Harrow & Wealdstone. The Bakerloo covers 14 miles and serves 25 stations.

Since the opening of the first part of the Bakerloo line in 1906, it has expanded, contracted and then expanded again to its present length. From its original northern terminus at Baker Street under the Metropolitan line station, it had expanded north to Queen's Park by 1915 and in stages to Watford by 1917. The Watford service used tracks built by the main line railway. In 1939 a new branch was built north of Baker Street which ran directly under the Metropolitan line to Finchley Road. At Finchley Road it rose to the surface and connected with the Metropolitan. This allowed Bakerloo trains to take over the Metropolitan's Stanmore service.

Until the opening of the Jubilee line in 1979 the Bakerloo operated both Stanmore and Watford services. However, the building of the new Jubilee tube from Charing Cross to Baker Street and its connection to the Stanmore branch of the Bakerloo line meant that the Bakerloo was confined to its Watford branch. In 1982 the Watford service was withdrawn and Queen's Park became the usual northern terminus once more. However, there were occasional journeys to and from Stonebridge Park to allow access to the new depot there and in 1984 some rush hour trips were extended to Harrow & Wealdstone. The present all-day service to Harrow & Wealdstone began in May 1988, Queen's Park remaining the Sunday terminus until October 1989.

The southern terminus of the Bakerloo is at Elephant & Castle, known to the staff simply as 'The Elephant'. Between the next station, Lambeth North, and Waterloo is a connection to London Road depot. This was once the main depot of the Bakerloo but is now only a stabling point for nine trains.

Originally named Trafalgar Square, the Bakerloo line platforms at the Charing Cross station complex were renovated when the Jubilee line was opened in 1979. The new image marked the end of the subdued finishes of previous decades, and heralded bold new designs which were to be a feature of 1980s station refurbishment schemes.

From Elephant to just south of Queen's Park the line is in tunnel. Among the features of interest along this part of the route are the sharply curved platform at Waterloo and the crossover at Piccadilly Circus. At Piccadilly, the two separate station tunnels become one at the northern end of the station where the crossover is located. Trains passing in both directions can be seen from either platform, an unusual sight in a tube station.

At Queen's Park, the line rises to the surface and uses two platforms between the two tracks on the Euston to Watford line. A small depot is provided which is unusual in being divided into two parts. At the south end there is a two-track shed capable of accommodating four trains. At the north end another four-berth shed is provided. This has four tracks, two sidings and two connecting tracks which allow Bakerloo trains access to the tracks to Watford. Bakerloo trains on trips north of Queen's Park have to pass through the shed, a unique experience for passengers on the Underground. At night, one of these tracks is used for stabling a seventh train.

Above The Bakerloo platforms at Piccadilly Circus offer a unique view on the network. The 'back to back' layout is itself unusual, but the single tunnel containing a crossover at the north end of the station allows passengers to see both platforms at once.

Right Regents Park was one of several Bakerloo line stations to be refurbished in 1989-90 using some new tiles to the original design, giving a very good impression of the way the stations looked in Edwardian times, although now with much brighter illumination. Note the large mirror on the headwall, giving the train operator a good view of the station at this straight and uncongested platform.

Left Many busy central London stations were renovated in the 1980s with bold new finishes, in all cases unique to one location. Many were finished in vitreous enamel panels, but Tottenham Court Road featured mosaic tiles to a design by Eduardo Paolozzi, appropriately busy for this frenetic station at the corner of Soho.

Below Few stations saw significant change when the Central line was extended over the former LNER route to Epping and Hainault after the second world war, but Loughton was an outstanding exception, with a new ticket hall and platforms. The then futuristic curved canopies reflected the optimism of the 'brave new world', but at the west end of the Central line they have already been replaced by more durable structures.

Central line

Ealing Broadway or West Ruislip to Hainault or Epping.
It covers 52 miles and serves 51 stations.

As first built in 1900 the Central line provided a cross-London route along the main east-west axis from the Bank to the western suburb of Shepherd's Bush. It was originally worked with locomotive-hauled trains but changed to multiple-unit traction in 1903. It was the first line to use multiple-unit control of trains. An extension to Ealing was opened in 1920.

The original traction system used a three-rail configuration having a centrally positioned positive current rail and the tunnels were slightly smaller in diameter than those subsequently adopted for later tube lines. The Central line therefore remained non-standard until its conversion to normal tube dimensions and the four-rail traction system in 1938-40. At the same time the original platforms were lengthened to take eight-car trains. Many of the station tunnels in the central area show evidence of the lengthening work undertaken at that time.

The eastern and western extensions of the line were begun in 1936 but were delayed by the war and not opened until 1946-49. At the eastern end of the line a large loop was formed partly by new tunnel construction and partly by taking over existing railways. Between Newbury Park and Wanstead the tunnels were used during the war to accommodate the manufacture of aircraft parts.

Many of the open-air stations at this end of the Central line were built in the nineteenth century by the Great Eastern Railway. Barkingside still has all its original buildings and contrasts sharply with those built in the 1940s like Wanstead, Loughton and Redbridge. The platforms at Redbridge are the shallowest on the tube lines, only 26ft below the road. From 1957 until closure in September 1994

Below Leyton is one of the stations at the eastern end of the line built by the Great Eastern Railway in Victorian times.

Right and below right Gants Hill was opened in 1948, although the design and much of the construction date from before the war. The long concourse between the platforms, similar to the elaborate stations on the Moscow Metro, gives the station a very spacious feel. A renovation and relighting programme in recent years has considerably enhanced the original appearance.

a single-track section of railway between Epping and Ongar was operated by Central line trains. Ongar remains, at present, the start point for measurement of the whole system, distance markers being provided every 200m all over the Underground providing reference points for operators and engineers.

The main line from Epping is joined at Woodford and Leytonstone by the two connections to the Hainault Loop. South of Leytonstone, Stratford is a major interchange.

At Bank, the next station west from Liverpool Street, interchange is provided with the Northern line, the Waterloo & City line, the Docklands Light Railway and with the District/Circle station at Monument. Bank has some very sharp curves which require quite severe speed reductions.

The straight route of the Central line over the central London section enables the 'hump profile' on which this and other tube lines were built to be seen clearly. Each station is approached on a rising gradient and left on a falling gradient to assist braking and acceleration respectively.

The line rises to the surface at White City. This station was built in 1947 to replace the original station which served the area which was known as Wood Lane. The approach to

the open section was via a sharp curve under Caxton Street known as the Caxton Curve. It has a radius of 400ft and originally formed part of a loop which allowed trains to leave Shepherd's Bush, rise to the surface station at Wood Lane and then return to Shepherd's Bush. The loop also allowed access to the depot. When the line was extended

Above The Central line platforms at Holborn were opened in 1933 to replace British Museum station, and provide interchange with the Piccadilly line for the first time. Today this is one of the system's busiest interchanges. Following a competition held in 1980, artist Allan Drummond was commissioned to design the station's new finishes, representing artefacts in the Museum. The work was completed in 1988.

Right The platforms at Marble Arch were given new finishes in the 1980s. This design, by Annabel Grey, depicts the famous Arch in a variety of different colours and decorative treatments and was completed in 1986. Here, it has been possible to incorporate the platform seats into the design as it progresses along the platforms.

to Ealing in 1920, the westbound line was on the right hand side of the eastbound because of the configuration of the loop. This situation still exists at White City. Access to the depot is now from the station instead of from the loop. Further west, the lines are crossed on a flyover to return to the standard British left hand running layout. Just west of North Acton station, another flyover provides a grade separated junction for the divergence of the Ealing

Broadway and West Ruislip branches. The branch to West Ruislip runs parallel to a Railtrack line and at Greenford and West Ruislip the stations are shared between Underground trains and those of Thames Trains and Chiltern Rail respectively. All the other stations are used by the Central line only. At Greenford, a small bay platform is provided between the Central line platforms to allow interchange between the Thames Trains shuttle service to Ealing Broadway and the

Above The Central line at Liverpool Street is a typical 1990s modernisation with large areas of white. Closed circuit television cameras are housed in the globe hanging from the ceiling.

Above right The line opened to Bank in 1900, when this was the eastern terminus. To avoid undermining buildings above the platforms were very sharply curved, causing problems of noise and large gaps between the platform and train which persist to this day. When the modernisation of the Central line was first planned in the mid 1980s, consideration was given to realignment, but the high cost ruled this out. The station was renovated over several years, and was not finished until 1998.

Right The gracefully curved canopy at Perivale station, completed in the late-1940s to the design of its previous owner, the Great Western Railway.

Underground. A feature unique to the Underground is that an escalator is provided to go up to the trains.

Refurbishment of the station platforms on the West Ruislip branch in recent times has included new canopies and waiting rooms. Between Ruislip Gardens and West Ruislip is a large depot. In accordance with the Underground's policy of always providing two exit tracks to each depot where possible, it has a connection to both

stations. A new permanent way depot has been provided adjacent to the main rolling stock depot and there is also a connection to the Metropolitan line at the rear of the depot.

West Ruislip station marks the western limit of the Central line and is the terminus of the Underground's longest possible continuous journey. It is 34.1 miles long and takes 1 hour 28½ minutes from Epping.

Circle line

Thirteen miles in length and serving 27 stations, the Circle line connects most of London's main line railway termini.

Almost all of the Circle line service is operated over the Metropolitan, Hammersmith & City and District lines. Only the short sections between High Street Kensington and Gloucester Road and between Aldgate and Minories Junction (east of Tower Hill) are used solely by Circle trains. The line's service is slotted between other lines' services, making it difficult to timetable and vulnerable to delays by other trains. Its normal service pattern requires seven trains per direction operating at 8 minute intervals on a 52½ minute round trip. At weekends and in the evenings the service widens to five trains per direction operating a 10 minute service on a 50 minute trip.

Facing page top Gloucester Road was opened in 1868, and was briefly the terminus of what is now the Circle line from High Street Kensington, before services were extended eastwards towards Westminster. The space above the station has been developed in recent years, and the opportunity taken to renovate the original Circle and District line platforms with cleaned brickwork and imaginative lighting.

Facing page bottom The 'C' stock for the Circle line was designed specifically for rapid alighting and boarding, and can clear surprisingly large numbers of people from busy platforms.

Below Bayswater dates from 1868, and is one of a number of Circle line stations retaining the original overall roof. The ticket hall and platform access stairs were expanded in 1998 to cater for the large numbers of people now using the station, but the short platforms here and at other stations between Paddington and High Street Kensington still restrict the length of trains which can be operated on the line.

Bottom When delivered, Circle line trains had almost all transverse seating, which failed to make the most effective use of the space available and discouraged people from moving away from the doorways. The layout changed when the trains were refurbished in 1990–93, and the previously hostile environment of cold efficiency was replaced by one of a bright, open and welcoming atmosphere.

One of the Circle line's peculiarities is the fact that the constant running of trains on a circular route used to cause problems with uneven wheel wear. To overcome this, one train per day is diverted from Tower Hill to Whitechapel, where it reverses and proceeds to Liverpool Street. This has the effect of turning the train round.

District line

Upminster in the east to Ealing, Richmond or Wimbledon with branches serving Edgware Road and Olympia.
The District covers 40 route miles and serves 60 stations.

The District line is one of the most complex of all the Underground lines and consequently difficult to operate. Its main section forms the southern part of the Circle line plus a single route eastwards to Barking and Upminster. In the west there is a trio of busy branches to Wimbledon, Ealing and Richmond. In addition, there is a shuttle service to Olympia and a Wimbledon service to Edgware Road. All these services pass through Earl's Court, which has become the hub of the line and the location of its control centre.

One of the main operating problems at Earl's Court is the passage of the Edgware Road service across the main line from the Wimbledon branch. A flyunder is provided for the westbound Ealing line to pass under the eastbound line from Wimbledon. A flyunder at the east end of the station allows trains from Edgware Road to pass under all the main line tracks.

The Wimbledon branch is served by trains from the main District line as well as those from Edgware Road. The stations between High Street Kensington and Edgware Road are able to accommodate only 6-car trains of C stock, not the longer 6-car D stock trains used on the rest of the District.

Facing page top Fulham Broadway was opened in 1880 as Walham Green, and is now known to thousands of fans as they make their way Chelsea's nearby football ground. The spacious platforms and ample access routes are ideal for the purpose, although this could not have been foreseen at the time, 25 years before the football club was formed!

Facing page bottom The island platform at Stamford Brook was constructed in 1912 to serve the District line branches to Richmond, Ealing and, at that time, Hounslow. When the Piccadilly line was extended westwards from Hammersmith in 1932, the side platform visible in the background was built on the new eastbound District line, leaving the island between the westbound District and Piccadilly lines. Trains on the Piccadilly do not normally stop.

At East Putney the District joins the Railtrack branch to Wimbledon. Special arrangements exist on Putney Bridge and between Turnham Green and Gunnersbury to separate the 4-rail LUL and 3-rail Railtrack current rail systems. These automatically ensure a supply to each train as it crosses from one system to the other but without allowing the train to 'bridge' the gap between the two. South West Trains does not run a regular passenger service over the line but uses it for access to the depot at Wimbledon Park. At Wimbledon, Underground trains use their own platforms to the west of those provided for national rail services. East Putney, Southfields and Wimbledon Park stations were owned and operated by British Rail until transferred to the Underground in April 1994 as a consequence of the privatisation of British Rail.

The line to Richmond (once part of the London & South Western Railway's Richmond to Kensington branch) is shared with trains operated by Silverlink working between Richmond and North Woolwich on the North London line. On its journey from Richmond the line crosses the River Thames at Kew. A similar crossing occurs at Putney Bridge on the Wimbledon branch and the District is the only Underground line to cross the Thames by bridge. At Gunnersbury the Silverlink service continues towards South Acton while the District route forms an impressive flying junction with the four-track District and Piccadilly lines at Turnham Green. The line from Gunnersbury to Richmond is owned by Railtrack.

Between Acton Town and Barons Court the Piccadilly line occupies the two centre tracks and the District the two outer tracks. The District stops at all stations while the Piccadilly normally runs non-stop between Hammersmith and Acton Town.

Stamford Brook has an unusual station layout which has four tracks but only three platforms. The two westbound tracks are served from an island platform dating from 1912 which used to be the District station for both directions. Originally, there was no platform for the remaining two tracks, which were part of a separate line connecting the Richmond branch with the Hammersmith & City line. When the Piccadilly line was extended westwards from Hammersmith in 1932 a new platform was provided at

Top The Underground is rightly proud of the rich architectural heritage it owns. Barons Court is an interesting example of an Edwardian station designed in a similar idiom to the many Leslie Green stations on 'tube' lines, but by a different architect – in this case Harry Ford. The 1906 ticket hall was renovated with great care for new ticketing technology in the late 1980s, with many original features retained.

Left Earl's Court is the hub of the various District line branches, through which all its services pass. The station is located in the heart of west London's bedsit land and in peak times passengers joining the system mingle on the platforms with those from further out changing trains to continue their journeys. The antique train indicators visible in the centre of the picture are an essential part of the 'listed' station and cannot be removed, although plans exist to supplement them with something more informative for today's customers.

Stamford Brook to serve what is now the eastbound District. The combination of the two platforms provides an interesting contrast in styles which has not been lessened by over 60 years of common ownership.

Near the east end of Ravenscourt Park, the next station towards London, the remains of the viaduct connecting the line to the H&C at Hammersmith can be seen. The District/Piccadilly tracks drop sharply at this point to pass under the centre of Hammersmith. The District/Piccadilly station at Hammersmith was completely rebuilt in the early 1990s but remains separate from the Hammersmith & City line station. A pedestrian subway connects the two.

Just east of Barons Court, the Piccadilly line enters its tunnel and runs below the District as far as South Kensington. The tunnel entrance is between the eastbound and westbound District tracks. Further east between West Kensington and Earl's Court there are two connections from the District, one to the Permanent Way depot at Lillie Bridge, the other to Olympia just before the underground junction with the Wimbledon branch.

Earl's Court, once described as the 'Crewe' of the Underground, handles five different District line services which split into three branches at the west end of the station and two at the east end. A few minutes' observation from one of the passenger footbridges over the platforms during the peak period shows just how complex the train service operation can be. The roof dates from 1878, whilst the Earl's Court Road entrance was rebuilt in 1906 in Leslie Green's standard style for the original stations on the Piccadilly, Bakerloo and Hampstead lines.

Once beyond Earl's Court, the line passes through Gloucester Road and South Kensington. Originally the District and Metropolitan each had their own tracks side by side until they were combined at a junction east of South Kensington. At this station there were originally four through platforms and two bays. The southernmost bay has now almost disappeared under the structure housing the Piccadilly line escalators which can be seen from the present westbound platform.

East of South Kensington the line is in shallow twin track tunnel (except for Whitechapel) as far as Bow Road. The gaps in the tunnel roof along this section are a reminder that operation was originally with steam locomotives. Above St James's Park station is the famous address '55 Broadway',

Right District line services were extended from Barking to Upminster in 1932, and a number of new intermediate stations built by the then London Midland and Scottish railway, which owned the Tilbury and Southend lines, to serve the expanding suburbs. Upminster Bridge is unique among these stations in that the railway is above street level, with steps down from the island platform to the booking hall.

Below The London, Tilbury and Southend Railway was driven out through London's East End in 1858 among densely packed streets of new housing. East Ham has always been was among the busiest of the new stations. District services were extended over the line as far as Barking in 1902, and the intermediate stations became the exclusive preserve of these trains in the late 1950s, with the electrification of the 'main line' services – although the stations continued in British Railways ownership for a further ten years.

headquarters of London Transport throughout its existence, and originally the site of the District Railway head office. Between this station and Victoria is the busiest section of the Underground, carrying over 40,000 passengers eastbound in a typical morning peak period.

Also of interest is the cross-platform interchange with the Central line at Mile End, the only example of tube and surface interchange at the same level in tunnel.

East of Bow Road the line rises steeply to the surface. This is the steepest gradient used by passenger trains on the Underground, at 3 per cent, although a steeper one exists at the Acton Town end of Ealing Common depot where the exit road is 3.6 per cent.

Beyond this point the line runs parallel with the former London, Tilbury & Southend line from Fenchurch Street. The c2c (formerly LTS Rail) 25kV electric trains run non-stop along this line except for a stop at Barking. District trains stop at all stations to Upminster. All four tracks along this route were originally owned by British Rail but now the District tracks are self-contained and all links with the fast tracks have been removed.

Some remnants of former links can be seen at Plaistow,

where a bay platform is used by some District and Hammersmith & City trains. On the north side of the line is a large car dealers' workshop which was the site of the Plaistow engine shed. At East Ham a disused bay can still be seen on the north side of the platform and beyond the station the c2c electric trains depot is built on the site of the former Underground depot. A major new interchange has been provided at West Ham to allow passengers access between the District and Jubilee lines, Silverlink and c2c services.

Two important stations on the eastern part of the District line, both shared with c2c, are at Barking and Upminster. Barking is a major interchange between various national rail routes and the Underground. Upminster is the easternmost station on the District and has a large depot beyond it, not visible from the platforms, built in 1958 to replace the old site at East Ham. At the other end of the line the main depot is at Ealing Common, built in 1905 for the electrification of the District Railway and formerly the workshop for the line as well.

Left Trains enter the twin bores of Brunel's Thames tunnel immediately after leaving Wapping station on the north shore of the river. Although strengthening works were carried out in the mid 1990s, the tunnel remains virtually as constructed in 1843 for pedestrians. Until the advent of the downstream tunnels for the Jubilee line and Docklands Light Railway in 1999, this was the lowest Thames crossing for trains.

Below The closure of the line in 1995 for the tunnel work gave the opportunity to refurbish the stations as well. The attractive panels at Shadwell serve also to conceal the water cascading down the walls, a perennial problem given the waterlogged soils the line traverses.

East London line

Whitechapel (Shoreditch in peak hours and Sunday mornings) to New Cross or New Cross Gate.
The line serves nine stations and covers five miles.

The East London line provides a service between the low-level platforms at Whitechapel and New Cross alternately with New Cross Gate. There is a small depot at New Cross. The service is extended to Shoreditch at peak times and on Sunday mornings. A feature of this line is that it utilises the tunnels built under the River Thames by Brunel. These consist of twin tunnels which were opened in 1843 for pedestrians. They were provided with rail tracks in 1869 and these were connected at the southern end to the London Brighton & South Coast Railway at New Cross. In 1876 a link was established at the northern end to the Great Eastern Railway just outside Liverpool Street station. The East London was electrified in 1913 and its passenger services were then operated by the Metropolitan Railway.

Right Canada Water station was built to provide interchange between the East London and Jubilee lines, and opened in 1999. The character of the station, with its wide platforms and generous circulating areas contrasts sharply with the other stations on the line. It is named after a nearby lake, one of few remnants of the once mighty Surrey Docks system.

Below The line runs through an area rich in London's seafaring history, and this has given plenty of inspiration when refurbishing the stations. Rotherhithe is at the south end of the Thames tunnel, and in the heyday of the docks the narrow platforms would have become very crowded.

The stations on the East London line have been improved and modernised in recent years. At Rotherhithe a pair of escalators has been installed under a curved transparent roof and the surface building restored. At Wapping, which is the deepest station (60ft) on the so-called sub-surface lines, the old lifts, installed in 1915, were replaced. At both Surrey Docks (renamed Surrey Quays in 1989) and Shadwell stations the surface buildings were replaced by new ones in 1983.

The entire line was closed in March 1995 for the Thames tunnel to be strengthened, and for general refurbishment. The Government 'listed' the tunnel on the eve of works starting, causing extensive delays while debate raged on the necessity for the work. In the event the refurbishment was carried out much as planned, but very late and with consequently increased cost and disruption. During the closure a new station was built at Canada Water to provide interchange with the extended Jubilee line. The East London re-opened in March 1998, with Canada Water following in August 1999.

Facing page At Edgware Road the line from Hammersmith meets the Circle line and the District line Wimbledon service. Trains of C stock operate all three routes.

Hammersmith & City line

Hammersmith to Barking.
This line serves 28 stations and covers 16½ miles.

In addition to sharing the Circle line's rolling stock, the Hammersmith & City line shares the route along the north side of the Circle, which is the oldest part of the Underground. The section from Hammersmith to Farringdon was built to accommodate the broad gauge trains operated by the Great Western Railway in the 19th century. This can still be detected today at places along the route which show generous spaces between tracks and in tunnels. West of Westbourne Park the tracks are further apart than needed today and many of the tunnel sections east of Edgware Road are much wider than sections built later.

The main depot for the Circle and Hammersmith stock is at Hammersmith. It was built for the electrification of the line in 1906 and has changed little since. It is located outside the station on the east side of the main line.

On the west side of the main line at Hammersmith an office block was built on the site of the former goods yard and, to accommodate additional stabling tracks should they ever be required, the block was constructed on a raised platform with pillars spaced to allow tracks to be laid between them. Further up on the same side there was a connection to the former London & South Western Railway's Kensington and Richmond line, over which the Metropolitan Railway operated services to Richmond via Turnham Green until 1906. This connection was removed in 1916.

At Westbourne Park, the H&C joins the national rail Great Western main line route into Paddington. There are no longer any track connections between the two railways but the H&C passes under the main lines and then runs parallel to them between Royal Oak and Paddington. The H&C platforms at Paddington are structurally part of the Railtrack station and are separate from the Circle line platforms. The H&C and Circle lines join at the junction at Praed Street before entering Edgware Road station. This is a four-

Westbourne Grove, with its fine Victorian station building and attractive red and yellow brickwork visible above the train.

platform station where the District line service to Wimbledon terminates. On the south side of the station (which is in a cutting) is Griffith House, one of a number of offices used by London Underground. The amount of railway property at this point is explained by the former presence of Metropolitan Railway steam locomotive and carriage depots and sidings.

Further along the line beyond King's Cross is a section where two extra tracks, known as the 'City Widened Lines', run parallel with the Underground line as far as Moorgate. These extra tracks were originally built by the Metropolitan Railway to allow local passenger and freight trains to run off the Midland and Great Northern Railways at King's Cross to Moorgate without conflicting with Metropolitan Railway services and to have a cross-London connection via Farringdon to the southern railway companies. Between King's Cross and Farringdon the Widened Lines cross under the H&C and Circle tracks.

In 1982, the Widened Lines were electrified at 25kV and disconnected from the Underground. In May 1988, the connection with the south London routes at Farringdon was reinstated after being disused for many years and new dual-voltage electric trains operated by Thameslink now provide a service between the Bedford line and several destinations south of the Thames with Underground interchanges at Farringdon, Blackfriars, London Bridge and Elephant & Castle.

At Moorgate and Aldgate facilities for reversing Metropolitan trains are provided in addition to the through tracks. Aldgate is located on the west leg of a triangle of lines connecting the Metropolitan, Circle and District lines.

At Aldgate East an interested observer at the west end of the station can watch the routes being changed for District and Metropolitan trains. Air-operated point machines are standard on the London Underground and these can clearly be heard operating here. The relationship between route setting, signal clearance and train movement is easily visible.

Towards the next station, Whitechapel, is a junction giving access to the East London line. There was originally a station here known as St Mary's, which was closed in 1938. Whitechapel is the terminus for some Hammersmith & City trains.

Below Green Park was once a relatively quiet station served only by the Piccadilly line, but with the advent of first the Victoria and then the Jubilee line, by 1979 it had become a busy interchange. The tiling used on this extension was far more colourful than on the Victoria line, and for the first time was supplied on pre-fabricated panels rather than the tiles being hung on site.

Bottom The first station at Dollis Hill was opened on the already well-established Metropolitan Railway in 1909 to serve new housing. The original structure was replaced by the current one for the opening of the Bakerloo service to Stanmore in 1939, and the whole branch transferred to the new Jubilee line almost forty years later. A Jubilee line train of 1996 tube stock is in the platform: a Metropolitan line train can be seen overtaking.

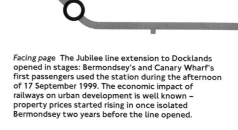

Facing page The Jubilee line extension to Docklands opened in stages: Bermondsey's and Canary Wharf's first passengers used the station during the afternoon of 17 September 1999. The economic impact of railways on urban development is well known – property prices started rising in once isolated Bermondsey two years before the line opened.

Jubilee line

Stanmore to Stratford; serves 27 stations in its 24 miles. It runs parallel with the Metropolitan line between Baker Street and Wembley Park.

The Jubilee line was opened to Charing Cross for public use on 1st May 1979. It was made up of two parts: a new tunnel section built between Baker Street and Charing Cross, plus that section of the Bakerloo line between Baker Street and Stanmore which had been worked by Bakerloo trains since 1939. Physical connections for trains as well as simple passenger interchange between the two lines are provided at Baker Street.

The northern end of the line between Stanmore and Wembley Park was opened in 1932 as a branch of the then Metropolitan Railway, most trains just shuttling to & fro, and connecting at Wembley with London services. Through services on the Bakerloo started in 1939, when a new tunnel was opened between Finchley Road and Baker Street.

The section south of Baker Street was opened in 1979 and terminated at Charing Cross, although the tunnels continued most of the way to Aldwych, where interchange with the now-closed Piccadilly line branch was planned by way of the intended alignment to Fleet Street, Fenchurch Street and thence to south east London. When the eastward extension was finally approved in 1993, however, market forces in the blossoming Docklands area drew the alignment across the Thames to serve the south bank with important interchanges at Waterloo and London Bridge (the former serving the classic stockbroker belt of Surrey and beyond), thence to the vibrant new financial centre at Canary Wharf, before swinging northwards to serve West Ham (interchange with District and Main Line services) and Stratford (connections to Essex and East Anglia). This enabled the line to tap in to almost all of the main line rail

routes giving access to the City, and feed the new Docklands area.

Diverging immediately south of Green Park, the new alignment has caused the short residual Charing Cross section to be abandoned. Further east, another diversion between Canary Wharf and Canning Town has moved the line across the river to the North Greenwich peninsula, adding a further two river crossings to the two that had already been planned. The peninsula was, in the 1990s, mostly wasteland, surviving closed gas works and dying industry, and the intention of the new station was to provide a large car park and bus interchange to serve transport-starved parts of south east London. After construction started the site was selected for the Millennium Dome, and this added much political pressure to open the extension in time for the celebrations, which it did.

The new tunnels are to a larger diameter than previous construction, providing space for a side walkway, and have comparatively sophisticated ventilation systems. Returning to the north shore of the Thames for the last time, the line passes through an impressive portal structure, reminiscent of the Thames Barrier, near the mouth of the Lea, to a station at Canning Town. This provides interchange with Silverlink's North Woolwich service, the Docklands Light Railway and local bus routes. The line then continues alongside the Silverlink line to Stratford, passing the new rolling stock depot at Stratford Market just before the terminus.

Left North Greenwich almost didn't happen, but a late change to the alignment took the Jubilee onto the Greenwich peninsula to help regenerate a derelict area, and afford a large 'park and ride' opportunity for south east London. The site is on the line of the Greenwich Meridian, and after construction had started it was selected for the location of the Millennium Dome and thus destined for fame – at least for the year 2000. With its blue glass finishes, this is arguably the best of a spectacular line of stations.

Below Part of the large circular station building at Canada Wharf seen from the upper escalator shaft to the platforms.

Below left Looking not unlike an airport terminal is the impressive station at Stratford.

The architecture of the stations on the extension can be described as spectacular. All have vast tracts of space, and project architect Roland Paoletti has employed world famous architects at the various stations resulting in a statement of importance not seen in the Underground since Charles Holden's designs of the 1930s. Canary Wharf is arguably the largest, although during construction Westminster was the country's deepest and most complex excavation – and with the District & Circle line station suspended perilously at the top and remaining in use throughout! At London Bridge the new ticket hall imaginatively uses the brick arches below the Railtrack station. All of the new below ground stations have platform edge doors to reduce the impact of draughts.

Stations on the rest of the line have a variety of styles ranging from late-1970s at Baker Street and south to Charing Cross, through late-1930s at Kilburn and Dollis Hill, early 1930s Metropolitan suburban at Kingsbury, Canons Park and Stanmore, to 1920s Metropolitan urban at Willesden Green and 1880 Metropolitan rural at Neasden.

Metropolitan line

Runs from Aldgate to Amersham, with branches to Chesham, Watford and Uxbridge with a total mileage of 41½ serving 34 stations.

The Metropolitan line is more suburban in character than the rest of the Underground and it has some semi-fast trains. Only the section south of Finchley Road is in tunnel; the remainder is in the open.

Originally the tunnel section had three stations between Finchley Road and Baker Street but these were closed in 1939-40 when the Bakerloo (now Jubilee) line was opened along the same route but in deep level tube tunnels. The sites of these disused stations can still clearly be seen as the trains make the steep climb up the gradient from Baker Street.

Baker Street station has seen much rebuilding over the years with the opening of the Jubilee line and the restoration work on Circle line platforms 5 and 6. The whole complex has a combination of 1860s restoration on the Circle, 1930s on the main station, 1970s on the Jubilee line platforms and 1980s on the Bakerloo platforms.

The tunnels between Finchley Road and Baker Street are, for the most part, in single track bores. This is because the first railway along the route was single-track only and doubled later. At Finchley Road the two Metropolitan tracks part to allow the Jubilee line tracks to emerge from the 1939 tube tunnel originally built for the Bakerloo extension from Baker Street. The Jubilee line serves the stations between

Finchley Road and Wembley Park which were operated by the Metropolitan before the 1939 changes. Now the Metropolitan trains normally run non-stop between these two stations. On the west side of the line runs the Chiltern Rail service to Marylebone.

At Neasden, on the east side of the Metropolitan line, is Neasden Depot. This is the main depot for the Metropolitan line and is the largest on the Underground, housing also part of the Jubilee line fleet. It was formerly the site of the Metropolitan Railway works, main depot and power station.

Facing page top The heart of the Metropolitan. Among London's first examples of commercial exploitation of a station site was Chiltern Court, a high class residential development by the Metropolitan Railway itself.

Facing page bottom Part of Baker Street station booking hall showing the glazed tile signing to the bookstall and refreshment rooms, as constructed by the Metropolitan Railway. With ten platforms, Baker Street station has the most on the Underground, of which four are for Metropolitan line services.

Below Hillingdon station had to be rebuilt to accommodate a diversion of the A40 trunk road, which went through the site of the original very basic buildings. Designed to offer a bright and airy atmosphere, the station was also the first specifically arranged with lifts to offer full step-free access to the platforms. It was opened in 1994.

After the depot was rebuilt to its present configuration in the late 1930s only a small steam shed was retained. This is still visible at the north end of the yard although the last steam locomotives were withdrawn in 1971. There has been much re-equipment of Neasden in recent years, including new automatic train washing machines and a new signalling system using solid state interlocking.

At Wembley Park, north of which the 1932 Metropolitan Railway Stanmore branch diverges, the signal box then installed and equipped with centralised train control still stands at the country end. The control equipment has long since been removed and Jubilee line tube trains now serve the branch, which still shows evidence of its origins. The station has had successive rebuildings to cope with traffic demands of the Wembley Exhibition of 1924-25, subsequent suburban growth and the crowds going to Wembley Stadium.

From here as far as Moor Park trains may run fast or stop at all stations as required, since four tracks are provided. At Harrow the configuration changes so that, instead of the slow tracks being between the two fast tracks as they are south of the station, north of the station they are east of the fast tracks. North of Harrow the fast tracks are shared with Chiltern trains to Aylesbury.

The north western suburbs of London served by the Metropolitan line were largely developed between the wars and owe much to the former Metropolitan Railway's astute combination of 'Metro-land' publicity, its policy of operating a separate land development company and its electrification and improvement of train services in this period. The Uxbridge line, which diverges north of Harrow-on-the-Hill, was built in 1904 and electrified with the main line to Baker Street in 1905. Further electrification from Harrow to Rickmansworth was completed in 1925 and, under the

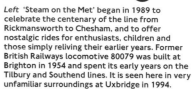

Left 'Steam on the Met' began in 1989 to celebrate the centenary of the line from Rickmansworth to Chesham, and to offer nostalgic rides for enthusiasts, children and those simply reliving their earlier years. Former British Railways locomotive 80079 was built at Brighton in 1954 and spent its early years on the Tilbury and Southend lines. It is seen here in very unfamiliar surroundings at Uxbridge in 1994.

Bottom The picturesque Watford branch – the Metropolitan soars above the Grand Union Canal near Croxley. Proposals exist to replace this section with a new link to Watford Junction.

London Transport regime, electric trains reached Amersham and Chesham in 1960.

The Uxbridge branch passes through an area intensively developed with suburban type estates in the 1930s, most of the houses being somewhat cheaper and smaller than those of the earlier Metro-land developments along the main line. Today only a few fields remain, at the western end, to remind the traveller what the whole area outwards from Willesden looked like before 1920. Most of the stations along this branch of the line follow the style produced for the Underground in the 1930s by Charles Holden, although other architects also had a hand in their detailed design; but Ruislip, which retains much of its 1904 appearance, offers a pleasant contrast.

At Rayners Lane the Metropolitan line is joined by the Piccadilly line branch from Acton Town. Some Piccadilly trains reverse at Rayners Lane using a centre siding provided west of the station. This is a typical example of the centre siding used all over the Underground and the observer on the platform can clearly see how it is used and how the signals operate to control it. Few other places offer such opportunities as many of the frequently used examples are in tunnels.

Between Ruislip and Ickenham there is a siding on the south side of the line. This is used both for reversing those Piccadilly line trains which terminate at Ruislip and as a transfer route for stock being moved to the Central line depot at West Ruislip. At Hillingdon, a striking new station was built in the 1990s.

At Uxbridge a set of sidings is provided on the north side of the station, where Metropolitan line trains are stabled overnight. The present station was built in 1938, the original station being now the site of the present sidings. There is a steep gradient into the station and the cutting walls gave considerable problems for a number of years. They had to be specially strengthened in 1954. The station itself is of particular interest. It has a three-track design with the centre track being provided with platforms on both sides. The roof has an interesting clerestory design very similar to that provided at Cockfosters. There is also a fine stained glass window overlooking the booking hall incorporating the coats of arms of Uxbridge Urban District Council and of Middlesex and Buckinghamshire Counties.

The line between Harrow and Moor Park was quadrupled in 1960-61 as part of the modernisation plan for the Metropolitan which included the electrification to

Amersham and the introduction of new rolling stock (the A stock) which is still in use on the line today. All the stations as far as Moor Park have platforms serving only the slow lines. Speeds over the fast lines of this section are higher than elsewhere on the Underground, 70mph being the permitted maximum. The grades are quite steep in some places however and this speed is rarely reached except between Northwood and Harrow.

Just north of Moor Park the short branch to Watford diverges to the right and the tracks are reduced to two from this point. The connections to the Watford branch form a triangle. Trains normally use the southern connection, proceeding from Moor Park to Watford.

The Watford branch was built in 1925 at the time of the electrification from Harrow to Rickmansworth. The station at Watford is about a mile away from the town centre but it serves a housing area known as Cassiobury Park. The line, which was expensive to build and produced disappointing traffic results, passes through a spectacular cutting at the approach to Croxley station and then high over a canal just outside Watford. It was originally intended to run the four tracks through to Rickmansworth and traces of the spaces levelled and bridge widths installed can be seen on the northbound or 'down' side of the line.

From Rickmansworth, the line climbs steeply through the Chiltern Hills to Amersham, now the most westerly point on the system. The whole area is quite rural but with scattered areas of development. At Chalfont & Latimer there is a single track branch to Chesham which is normally operated by a single unit of A stock shuttling between the two places. At peak times two through trains operate while the shuttle train is held in the short terminal platform at Chalfont.

The Metropolitan line now terminates at Amersham but a service continues to Aylesbury provided by Chiltern Rail. The station has three platforms, expanded from the simple two-track station of the conventional type originally provided. North of the station a pair of reversing sidings is provided for Metropolitan trains. The normal Metropolitan service to this point is half-hourly and is supplemented by an hourly service to Aylesbury from Marylebone.

Below Clapham North station was once typical of the City & South London railway: Euston and Angel were rebuilt in 1968 and 1992 respectively, leaving just this and Clapham Common today. Careful management is needed to prevent overcrowding at these platforms, and consideration has been given to ways of replacing them.

Northern line

Morden to Edgware, Mill Hill East or High Barnet via Bank or Charing Cross; serves 51 stations and 36 route miles.

The Northern line possesses the longest section of continuous tunnel on the system, 17 miles 528 yards between Morden and East Finchley (via Bank). For many years this was the longest railway tunnel in the world.

The line has two main routes across London. Each was originally a separate railway – the City & South London (C&SLR), today's Bank branch, and the Hampstead & Highgate (now the Charing Cross branch). The C&SLR tunnels were built to a small diameter, and these had to be enlarged in the 1920s to match the tunnel diameter of the other tube lines. Some stations show variations in tunnel diameter where platforms were extended to accommodate longer trains.

In some areas traces of the old arrangements still exist. At Clapham North and Clapham Common there is a narrow island platform in a single large station tunnel accommodating both tracks. A similar layout existed at Angel until mid-1992, when a new station opened at a cost of over £70 million. A dramatic traffic increase had rendered the old layout potentially unsafe.

At Euston (southbound City platform) the former C&SLR terminus tunnel originally accommodated two tracks and an island platform. Now it serves only one track and like Angel has a wide platform.

Below Designs for Oval station to be refurbished with a cricket theme (to reflect the Surrey Cricket Club ground giving the station its name) were commissioned several years before the final scheme was realised in 1997, but delayed by a shortage of funds.

Right Most stations on the original 'Yerkes' tubes (Bakerloo, Piccadilly and Northern) had their names included in the tiled platform finishes, before the potential of platform wall advertising was realised. The deepest station below the surface was to have been called Heath Street, but was actually known as Hampstead from the outset. The original tiling has been revealed by recent refurbishment work.

Bottom right Not as old as it looks – the original atmosphere of Mornington Crescent was restored during the station's closure for lift replacement in the mid 1990s. Most people know the station more for the radio panel game based on it than anything else.

Further south over a section of the line between Bank and Borough the original tunnels were crossed over for ease of construction and led to the station tracks having 'right hand running' instead of the normal left handed arrangement. This arrangement may also be seen at White City, Central line and on the Victoria line at Warren Street and King's Cross.

At London Bridge the southbound track was diverted in 1997 to serve a new platform in a similar manner to the work at Angel. The station had suffered from very congested access arrangements, and the diversion enabled the disused southbound platform to provide a new concourse, with additional routes to the surface and to the Jubilee line.

At each end of the City section there is a junction with the West End branch. At Camden Town the connection is a series of underground tunnels which allow trains to run from either the City or the West End to either of the north London branches of the line. One serves Edgware via Golders Green, the other High Barnet and Mill Hill East via Finchley Central.

There is a simpler junction at Kennington. Here a reversing loop (for Charing Cross branch trains) and siding are provided and the line continues south to Morden, the southernmost point on the system.

A variety of services can operate on the Northern line. Trains going north from Morden may run via Bank or Charing Cross to Edgware or to High Barnet or Mill Hill East, a uniquely complex operation for a tube line. At both Camden Town and Kennington there are two platforms for each branch. Cross-platform interchange is provided for City and West End trains at the latter.

The line south of Clapham Common was extended to Morden in 1926 and the surface stations along this section are in a standard pattern of Portland stone evolved by Charles Holden, easily adaptable to varying site conformations and designed to show up well when floodlit at night. The whole of this section is in tunnel except for the

terminus at Morden. Beyond the station is Morden depot. Although Morden houses many trains overnight, Golders Green is the main maintenance centre. This was the site of the original terminus of the Charing Cross, Euston and Hampstead Railway when it opened in 1907.

The CC,E&H Railway originally ran from Charing Cross to Golders Green with a branch to Highgate (the present Archway station). It was extended to a terminal loop at Embankment in 1914, which became disused when the line was extended south to Kennington to meet the enlarged City & South London Railway in 1926. The present sharply curved northbound platform at Embankment is located on the former loop. This platform was the origin of the system of automatic warning lights and a recorded 'Mind the gap' message now found at many curved platforms.

Floodgates were provided at Embankment in 1939 where they could be used to close off the under river tunnels should they be breached by bomb damage. Floodgates are also provided at other vulnerable points on deep level and sub-surface lines but few are now needed.

The Northern line has the deepest station below street level on the system. This is Hampstead, which is 192ft below the surface. Special high speed lifts are provided here, since it is too deep to provide escalators at a reasonable cost. Just north of the station the Underground

is at its deepest — 221ft below the surface of Hampstead Heath. Not only does the line have the deepest lifts on the Underground but also the longest escalators. These are at Angel, rebuilt in 1992, and have a vertical rise of 90 ft.

At Golders Green the line reaches the surface and has access to the main depot which lies adjacent to the station. The depot buildings are typical of the 1905-7 style adopted for the original electrification depots and are similar to those at Ealing Common, Lillie Bridge and London Road. Unfortunately, the depot at Golders Green was originally designed for five-car trains. The line now uses seven-car

Left The Northern line platforms at Tottenham Court Road complement those on the Central (p 36), but with a black frieze to reflect the line colour.

Below left Charing Cross was the last of twelve crosses erected at the resting places of the funeral cortege of Queen Eleanor, wife of King Edward I, en route from Nottinghamshire to Westminster Abbey in 1290. The event is commemorated in the effective black & white mural on the Northern line platforms of that station.

Right Angel station was rebuilt and re-opened in 1992, with a new ticket hall and escalators. The northbound track was diverted to serve this new platform, enabling the original island platform to be converted for southbound use only.

Below The terminus at High Barnet, retaining its country branch look.

Bottom right When the Underground was extended to East Finchley, a new station was built to replace the GNR original. Two island platforms were constructed, the outer tracks serving the tunnels to Camden Town.

trains and some tracks in the depot cannot take a full length train, making it difficult to operate. The building boom which took place in the area immediately after the line was opened has effectively precluded any expansion of the site.

North of Golders Green the line is in the open except for a short tunnel at the Burroughs near Hendon. It is interesting to follow the line on foot between Golders Green and Brent Cross stations to examine how in 1923, a victim of its own success, it had to be projected through an area already covered with new houses, some of which had to be

demolished. At Brent Cross there were originally passing loops on each side of the station but these have been removed. At Edgware there are stabling sidings next to the terminus and there are still traces of the work done in preparation for an extension to Elstree abandoned at the beginning of the second world war.

The other branch of the Northern line goes north from Camden Town to Finchley Central, where the line splits. A single track serves the short branch to Mill Hill East while the main line continues along the very attractive route to High Barnet. The branch to High Barnet was taken over from the

main line railway in 1940 and the stations still retain the characteristics of their original owner, the Great Northern Railway. The line to Mill Hill East has an attractive brick arch viaduct over Dollis Road where the Underground reaches its highest level above ground at 60ft.

For the extension to Mill Hill East and High Barnet a small depot was built at Highgate including some sidings at the side of Highgate Wood.

Mornington Crescent station was closed in mid 1992 to carry out lift replacement and a renovation scheme, but work was suspended by the end of the year through funding difficulties, delaying the reopening until April 1998.

Right Gillespie Road was the penultimate stop on the original line to Finsbury Park, and the only one to give access to the shallow platforms by means of a ramped subway rather than by lift. The Arsenal football club moved here from Woolwich in 1913, and had gained enough importance for the station to be renamed in 1932 – the only case of a station named after a football club.

Below Once the western terminus of the Piccadilly, Hammersmith station was rebuilt in 1932 when the line was extended further, and again through the mid 1990s as part of a property development. Cross-platform interchange is provided between the Piccadilly and District lines, with lift access to street level and the integral bus station.

Piccadilly line

Cockfosters to Heathrow Airport or Uxbridge. The line covers 44 miles and serves 52 stations.

The Great Northern, Piccadilly & Brompton Railway, later known as the Piccadilly line, opened in 1906 between Hammersmith and Finsbury Park. The extensions at each end were largely undertaken during the 1930s. The Piccadilly serves Heathrow Airport using the extensions completed to Heathrow Central (Terminals 1/2/3) in 1977 and by a single-track loop to Terminal 4 in 1986. The platforms on the sections of line used by both Piccadilly tube trains and District surface stock trains have to be a compromise height to allow a reasonable step between either type of train and the platform. Stations between Acton Town and Hounslow Central also have platforms of this height. Until 1964 these too were shared with the District line.

Left Sudbury Town was rebuilt in 1931 as a prototype for the now famous designs on the extended Piccadilly line. It replaced a simple structure built by the District Railway with the line to South Harrow in 1903.

Below The architecture of Barons Court, opened in 1905, is very different to Hammersmith 'next door'. The station had been rebuilt in preparation for the arrival of the Piccadilly line, using the centre tracks, the following year.

The Piccadilly line from Heathrow passes the line's main rolling stock depot at Northfields and is then provided with four tracks east from there. The eastbound fast track between Northfields and Acton Town is fitted with water sprays which can be used for braking and adhesion trials for any of the Underground's trains.

At Acton Town, the Uxbridge/Rayners Lane route, combined with the District's Ealing Broadway branch, meets the line from Heathrow. Here Piccadilly line trains are diverted to the two centre fast tracks for the non-stop trip to Hammersmith. Late at night and early in the morning they call additionally at Turnham Green.

Hounslow West, until 1975 the terminus of the branch, now has its 1920s ticket hall connected to below-ground platforms built fifty years later. Other station buildings of interest on this branch are at Hounslow Central, dating from 1912, and Osterley, Boston Manor and Northfields, all built in the 1930s.

Right Arnos Grove station, regarded by many as perhaps the classic Holden design, is less well known at platform level. The heavy concrete structures have lasted longer than more recent – and elegant – styles, and little has changed in this view since it was new in 1932. Arnos Grove has three tracks between two island platforms, and is the terminus for some trains.

Below The ticket hall of Northfields is typical of this generation of Piccadilly line stations, offering light and space. Many were originally built with uplighters which were then removed. Several, including Northfields, were replaced in a programme of sensitive renovation work in the late 1990s.

The line is in tunnel between Barons Court and Arnos Grove. Of interest along this section is the Leicester Square to Covent Garden portion of the line, which represents the shortest distance between stations on any line (0.16 miles). Between Covent Garden and Holborn the line swings sharply northwards where two separately planned railways became one. At King's Cross there is a single line connection between the eastbound Piccadilly line and the northbound Northern line. Built in 1927, this is the only connection available between the Northern line and the rest of the Underground for stock transfer purposes.

At Finsbury Park there are connections between both tracks of the Piccadilly line and the Victoria line as well as cross-platform interchange. It is occasionally possible to compare the stopping sequence of the automatic Victoria line train with the manual stop of the Piccadilly train when two trains arrive together. At Arnos Grove, the first in the open, there is a three-track station with the centre track having a platform on each side.

Southgate is an unusual station in that it has the only tube tunnel platform on the Underground from which the end of the tube tunnels can be seen. The next station north is Oakwood, which has a connection at its north end to Cockfosters depot. Oakwood station, like all the Piccadilly stations built for the northward extension of the line from its original terminus at Finsbury Park, is in the 1930s style of Charles Holden. Many of these designs are now so highly regarded as specimens of the best public architecture of the period that they have become protected structures.

Left Few stations now have the escalator uplighters left, which were almost universally fitted in the 1930s. They have been retained at Southgate, along with the daffodil-shaped concourse uplighters (known to staff as 'the daffs'), partly obscured in this view by more recent signage.

Below The Piccadilly line was extended to Heathrow Central, now called Heathrow Terminals 1, 2 & 3 in 1977. Few trains now terminate here, but most pause on their way to London from Terminal 4, using either platform face.

Victoria line

Walthamstow Central to Brixton; serves 16 stations and is 14 miles in length.
It is all in tunnel except for Northumberland Park depot.

The Victoria line was the first completely new tube line to be built across central London since the tube building boom of 1905-7 and it rapidly became one of the most heavily used lines on the network. It was opened from Walthamstow to Highbury & Islington in September 1968, to Warren Street in December that year, to Victoria in March 1969 and to Brixton in July 1971. It was designed to relieve congestion in the north-east to West End corridor.

From its opening, Automatic Train Operation has been employed on the line. Acceleration, signal checks and station stops are all performed automatically.

The nature of the subsoil south of the Thames makes tunnelling particularly difficult and expensive. The Victoria line extension to Brixton was the first extension of the tube into south London since the Northern line's extension to Morden in the mid-1920s. An important design objective was the avoidance of curves below 20 chains radius, allowing higher speeds than average on the system.

The design of the route also incorporated many cross platform interchanges. Some involved special diversions. At Finsbury Park, the former westbound Piccadilly platform became the northbound Victoria line tunnel and in the opposite direction both lines used the former Northern City line platforms, where ceilings are higher than usual in a tube station. The Northern City line originally ran between Finsbury Park and Moorgate but was curtailed at Drayton Park when construction work at Finsbury Park started. In

Below The new trains for the Victoria line were the first to be styled by an artistic designer – Professor Misha Black – rather than an engineer, and perhaps typify the 1960s. This line-up is seen at Northumberland Park depot, the only part of the line not in tunnel.

Left Each of the new Victoria line stations designed in the 1960s had its grey tiled walls relieved by coloured tile panels by different artists – Blackhorse Road is among the more obvious results. At stations beyond Finsbury Park the tunnel structure, as here, was not lined with decorative ceiling panels and always looked a little gloomy as a result.

1975 the line was taken over by British Rail for incorporation into its Great Northern electrification scheme. Cross platform interchange between it and the Victoria line is provided at Highbury & Islington, where reconstruction like that at Finsbury Park was undertaken.

South of Highbury the Victoria line tunnels cross to give right-hand running. This allows cross platform interchange at Euston with the City branch of the Northern line. This was another site which involved diversion of existing routes. South of Warren Street the tunnels again cross to regain left hand running.

Cross platform interchange with the Bakerloo is provided at Oxford Circus and with the Northern at Stockwell but at Green Park and Victoria the line is at a different level from that of other lines. Victoria has a pair of reversing sidings beyond the station and at Brixton and Walthamstow two stabling sidings are provided beyond the termini.

Waterloo & City line

Waterloo to Bank, with no intermediate stations. Length 1½ miles.

This short railway was London's second tube line, having opened in 1898. It was the brainchild of the London & South Western Railway which by the end of the nineteenth century was already becoming an important commuter route but which, like most of its rivals, was unable to reach the City; then a proportionately more important employment centre than now.

The original wooden-bodied trains survived until 1940 when they were replaced by specially designed tube-sized cars embodying the relatively unrefined technology of the Southern Railway's surface stocks, which had been superseded on the Underground several years earlier. These trains were themselves to survive until 1993, some cars to the end bearing 'Southern Railway' motifs inside, recalling pre-nationalisation days of the early 1940s.

In 1993 the line closed for several weeks for some remaining civil engineering works and resignalling to take place. When it reopened on 19th July 1993, it was equipped with new trains; in effect units of Central line 1992 tube stock added to the Underground order and sold on to Network SouthEast, the only significant difference being in external livery (shown above).

The line is wholly in tunnel and physically isolated from all other railways. Until 1990 cars were moved to and from the line by hydraulic lift at Waterloo. This facility had to be removed as part of the preparations for the international platforms for Eurostar services, and the 1940 cars and their replacements had to be lifted by mobile crane.

Uniquely amongst London's tube lines, the Waterloo & City (or 'Drain') remained outside London Transport ownership when LT was formed in 1933.

In April 1994 however, with the impending privatisation of British Rail, the line was transferred to London Underground.

![Underground logo] Operation

Some of the highest risks of accident arise around the platform-train interface. 1995 and 1996 tube stocks have been fitted with stiff rubber 'buffers' at the carbody ends to reduce the size of the gap – and thus the risk of falling – while earlier trains have been fitted with flexible inter-car barriers to eliminate the gap altogether.

Safety

The operation of railways in Britain is governed by the production of a Safety Case, which sets out in detail how the railway is to be operated and managed, and which has to be approved by the Railway Inspectorate, a branch of the government's Health & Safety Executive. This ensures not only that safe practices, materials and equipment are used on the railway itself, but also that staff are properly trained and licensed for the tasks they have to perform, and all decisions take into account the impact on safety.

Since the 1980s the Underground has used risk analysis techniques to understand the level of hazards, and to systematically increase safety. The effect has been to reduce accidents on an already safe facility still further, and enhance the Underground's position as the safest form of transport in Britain.

Signalling

On most lines, signalling is by means of two-aspect colour lights on lineside signals – green for proceed and red for stop. Where visibility of a signal is restricted – for example on a curve – a repeater is provided, which will display a yellow aspect to warn of a red signal ahead. On the fast sections of the Metropolitan line, yellow is also used on normal running signals to give the driver longer warning of the need to slow down. Whenever a signal is red, a 'trainstop' located alongside the track is raised, which contacts a lever (connected to a 'tripcock') on any train which attempts to go past, causing an emergency brake application. The layout of the signals is such that any train in this position would be brought to a stand before it collided with a train in the next section.

The signals are operated automatically – a low voltage current is passed through the running rails, which maintains the signal at green. When a train enters the section and short circuits the current, the signal turns red. In areas where the signals need to be controlled manually, including junction areas, this is achieved either by levers in a local signal box, or more normally remotely from a control room. Signals at junction areas are interlocked with each other to prevent conflicting moves being cleared, and with points so that they are proved to be fully set and locked in the desired position before the signal can be cleared.

Over the years, there have been increasing levels of automation of route setting, so that a move once requiring the operation of several levers can now be achieved by, perhaps, the pushing of a single button or without manual intervention at all. The safety interlocking has always remained at local level, originally by retaining the mechanical locking bars used in signal cabins from the very earliest days of the railways, but since the mid-1980s through a fail-safe form of computer-proving, known as 'solid state interlocking'. The first such site was at Northolt on the Central line. A method of operating these sites by remote control developed in the 1950s was the use of 'programme

Left The need for tight operational control and passenger security has led to the provision of sophisticated control rooms at stations, giving a comprehensive view of all areas, and status indications of the various items of equipment.

machines' – mechanical devices using a wide plastic roll containing timetable data in the form of punched holes. The idea was novel at the time, but although very many of these remain in use today, their operation is too inflexible for the high intensity and quality of service demanded now.

In the early 1970s, a trial was conducted at Rickmansworth signal box to use a computer for the control of the Watford area. This was successful, and a major installation took place in 1982 at the north end of the Piccadilly line. Although that installation caused problems at the outset (and to a degree still does), lessons were learned, and more areas used the same form of control, most notably the Bakerloo line south of Queen's Park in 1989.

By this time, the railway industry was alert to the safety benefits of automatic train protection (ATP), first used by the Underground on the Victoria line in 1968, but also valuable on manually-driven services and initiated on the Central line in 1998. In normal signalling, once a train has passed the green signal it is free to continue, whereas under ATP conditions it requires a constant 'proceed' signal or it will stop. Several systems were developed around the world, some linked to transmission-based signalling. A disadvantage of conventional fixed sections is that no train can enter an area until the preceding one has left the following one – thus trains are a minimum of two sections apart. In a transmission-based system the protected area behind a train moves along with it, enabling trains to be spaced much closer together, but in complete safety.

Way back, the Underground realised the potential advantages of automatic train operation as well (ATO). This is a separate system from safety signalling, and is still governed by that equipment, but replaces the need for the driver to accelerate and stop the train. Trials on the Underground started on a small section of the District line in the early 1960s, and were sufficiently successful to progress to full scale trials on the Hainault–Woodford section of the Central (then operated as a separate service), and for the Victoria line from its inception in 1968.

Communications

Fixed sites have been able to communicate by telephone for over 100 years, but this has not been helpful for trains, which used to have to stop so that the driver could connect his handset to the bare copper wires provided along the tunnels. There was no way for the controller to contact a driver, other than sending station staff to wait for the train – time consuming and not very useful if the train failed to arrive!

Radio systems came surprisingly late to the network, but had revolutionised control techniques by the 1980s and allowed one-person operation. Improving technology will soon be tapped by the 'Connect' Private Finance Initiative (PFI), which will allow virtually any voice or data transmission to take place between all sites, be they fixed or moving. Apart from enabling simultaneous conversation between drivers and other staff, and giving mobile staff additional security it will also permit a depot to receive real-time information about any defects on trains in service. The provision will largely be funded through the sale of transmission capacity on the network to third parties, exploiting the superb routeways offered around London by tube tunnels.

As well as operational communication, it will be possible to provide customers with far better information about services, both on the network, and elsewhere through internet and the other media.

The opening of the Jubilee line extension almost doubled the Underground's stock of escalators. Canary Wharf alone has twenty.

Lifts and escalators

The means of getting to and from the platforms are as important as the trains themselves. The earliest stations, in shallow tunnels, used only stairs, but the advent of tube construction in 1890 necessitated some mechanical assistance, and lifts were provided – initially hydraulically powered, but soon mechanical winding was used instead.

The problem with lifts is that they can take only a limited load, and then only in discrete batches. Even while the tubes were still much quieter than now, this began to cause problems, and in 1911 the first escalator was installed at Earl's Court. By the 1920s the machine had developed into its current form, with a straight step off at the landings rather than the 'shunt' requiring a sideways step at the end. Over the next few years escalators spread widely across the network, often involving considerable station reconstruction. Lifts were retained at a number of stations, however, the deepest being at Hampstead (55 metres).

Although escalators are good at carrying large numbers of people, they are less suitable for those who may be unfit, or with luggage, children and so on. Enlightened attitudes towards disabled people – and the recognition that a very large potential market was being disadvantaged – led a trend back to providing lifts, but this time to supplement rather than replace escalators. All new and substantially reconstructed stations will ensure, by lifts if necessary, that access between street and platforms is step-free.

Track

The Underground had normally used 95lb/yard bullhead rail, but this offers little inherent stiffness and in the interests of good maintenance and smooth running, heavier flat bottomed rail is now progressively being laid. Work on the long programme of completely replacing the track, and its bed, is slowly progressing, but because of disruption (a weekend shutdown is usually necessary to replace a section of track) and cost, currently estimated at about £2 billion, this is having to be spread over many years. The work includes the replacement of the old limestone ballast with granite – more expensive, but far longer lasting. Often, track renewal has to be preceded by the stabilisation of earthworks and reconstruction of drains, so even on a short section the work may have to be spread over a year or so to allow new formations to stabilise. Routine track and lineside maintenance has to be carried out in the few hours when trains are not running – often less than four hours' work is possible once the site has been reached. Much of this work is locally based, but materials and heavy machinery are stored at the depots at Ruislip and Lillie Bridge (near West Kensington).

County Council tram power station), Lots Road (Chelsea) and Neasden. The latter was closed in due course, and bulk power obtained from the National Grid, but the other stations continued, gradually becoming less dependable. In the end, both were capable of using either natural gas or oil, Lots Road provided the base supply while Greenwich was added for peak and emergency loads. In August 1998 a PFI deal was implemented with a consortium including Seeboard, once the nationalised local Electricity Board for south east England, for the supply and distribution of high tension electricity, initially using the existing generating plant at Greenwich and distribution network.

Ticketing

Tickets on the Underground are magnetically-encoded and of credit card size, whatever their availability. They can be purchased at Underground and National Rail stations, either from the ticket office (though these are not always open at many stations) or ticket machines. Travelcards (unlimited travel tickets for a set period) can be bought as well from agents – usually small shops – and by telephone order.

Under the 'Prestige' PFI deal awarded in 1998, improved ticket machines are being installed, more customer-friendly than earlier examples and capable of accepting credit cards. At Heathrow and possibly other locations foreign currency acceptance is also intended. Early versions of the new generation of machines were commissioned airside at Heathrow Terminal 1 in 1997, Westminster in 1998 and at other Jubilee extension stations in 1999.

The next stage of Prestige will be the introduction of contactless smartcards from August 2002. These will replace many magnetic stripe tickets and will allow quick development of the ticket range to meet the changing travel patterns and needs of customers. It will also accelerate and improve financial and management information for the Underground and its fellow operators.

Power

Energy is supplied through the third and fourth rails at a nominal 630 volts dc, the insulated return originally selected by the District and Metropolitan Railways to avoid corrosion. This leaves a legacy of very cluttered track – difficult for staff and customers, should detrainment be necessary, and expensive to maintain. The possibility of using a technically more modern system has been debated on a number of occasions but no firm plans exist for a change.

When the national power industry was nationalised in 1948 the Underground was deliberately left out to ensure security of supply, most of the energy coming from the company's own plant at Greenwich (a former London

 # Future

Helped by London's buoyant economy and improving quality of its own service the Underground has experienced growth in demand for a number of years. This trend is forecast to continue for at least the first two decades of the 21st century. As consumers we are more demanding than our predecessors: we are less likely to tolerate crowding, unpredictable journey times or unpleasant surroundings, and we try to look after the less able members of society better than before. We are also fondly attached to our cars and will need, as a minimum, an integrated transport system as we complete our journey. The move toward the relative security of funding offered by the Public-Private Partnership (PPP) process, the recognition that the private car has to be restricted, the sharp focus of the new Greater London Authority, and the anticipated vibrant future for London's commercial activity all auger well for the Underground. Thus London Underground has confidently drawn up plans for the next twenty years, which spell out improved travelling conditions for all customers.

Integration

The process of integrating Underground, National rail, bus and other services through good physical links, comprehensive information and through-ticketing has been continued in London since before the inception of London Transport in 1933, but lost momentum in the 1980s as a result of government policy. Recent developments at North Greenwich (Underground, bus and massive car park) and

Canning Town (Underground, National rail, Docklands Light Rail, bus), added to similarly user-friendly interchanges at Stratford, Edgware, Hammersmith and Harrow in past years, all represent excellent improvements for users. Turnpike Lane is due to be added to the list in the near future.

The best of these facilities involve considerable liaison with local authorities and developers to provide transport interchange linked with shopping centres, office and residential development. There are many signs that these external agencies now take public transport provision very seriously, and some very exciting potential developments are under consideration at White City/Shepherd's Bush and at Park Royal, the latter providing a new station on the Central line and interchange with the Piccadilly. The proposal by Railtrack to provide the asset base for the subsurface lines, announced by the Government in June 1999, opened the possibility of taking integration further by running main line trains on the north side of the Circle line.

New communications links will provide the opportunity for better real-time information about services around the network – for example the display of bus countdown information within Underground stations, but also the availability of advice and information to homes and the workplace through the internet. Smartcard tickets will additionally allow ticket products to match individual customer needs far more closely than now, and a combination of telephone sales, started in 1999, and greater availability of 'high street' outlets will reduce the need to join a queue at the station.

A wider audience

There have been considerable advances in the understanding of needs of those who are less than fully mobile, whether by disability or because they are accompanied by children, luggage or whatever. This group includes all of us at some time, and represents a very large number of people. The provision of inductive loops for the deaf, tactile and radio beacon guidance for the blind, and lifts to change levels have all begun. The opening of the Jubilee line into Docklands has, together with a number of other stations equipped with lifts, provided access for all to a core part of the system including both stations at Heathrow Airport.

Reliably faster journeys

Already, local plans are being implemented as short term actions to improve journey time, and the reliability of services. These range from improved ways of managing the service to significant physical works. An example of the latter was the closure of part of the Northern line's City branch in the summer of 1999 to enable tunnel and track alignment to be improved at five separate locations between Kennington and Moorgate, and thus remove permanent speed restrictions which had applied here from the outset. The consequence is improved journey times, a more comfortable ride and greater regularity.

Less spectacular is the ongoing work of strengthening embankments and cuttings, replacing bridges and drains, and replacing track with modern formations. The availability of funding through the PPP process in future will allow the backlog accumulated in the past through underfunding to be addressed, and piece by piece will result in faster and smoother rides.

Equally important is the railway's signalling. The Central and extended Jubilee lines were to have signalling systems to allow automatic operation and frequencies of 33-35 trains per hour (tph), but the supplier failed to achieve this on the extended Jubilee line. Once delivered, the new signalling will offer significantly more frequent services than at present. Control centres for the new systems are provided respectively at White City and Neasden.

On the District and Piccadilly lines, the central control system based at Earl's Court, which operates local signalling in the junction areas, is well past life expectation and a rolling project is under way to achieve more flexible, and far more reliable, control. For the Piccadilly line, area signalling control will be provided at the 'new' operations and maintenance centres built in the late 1990s at Arnos Grove and Acton Town, with a centrally-located co-ordination point (though all functions will be possible from any site). The District line is considering Tower Hill as the location of a new facility to replace Earl's Court.

The Northern line has plans to introduce new signalling to increase frequencies, improve junction management and thus fully exploit the capability of the new trains to accelerate the service.

Increasing train service capacity

Given the forecast increase in demand, plans now exist for capacity to be increased on all lines. The Northern, Central and Jubilee lines have been referred to above; and planned for the early years of the new decade are interim improvements for the Piccadilly line, to allow a high reliability 30tph service. The main elements are the easement of known bottlenecks in the signalling system, the provision of additional reversing capacity at the north end of the line and the availability of additional trains. The

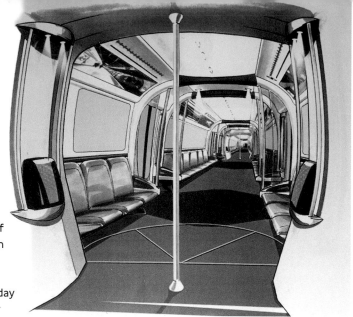

Right Ideas are being formulated for the next generation of trains. When the time comes for these to be built, a more spacious interior is planned, probably with wide door-free connection between cars.

latter need is addressed by the rebuilding of 16 trains of 1983 stock displaced from the Jubilee line in 1998. Even more spectacular is the proposed provision of new platforms at Oakwood and Cockfosters to remove the inflexibility this end of the line imposes on today's 'all day peak' service, and allow the expansion anticipated over the next few years.

The Victoria line is due for a complete upgrade in a few years' time. The trains and signalling fall due for normal renewal between 2005 and 2009, but anyone using the line will know that the current level of service, good as it is, falls woefully short of demand for most of the week. One solution is to equip the line for frequencies as high as 36tph. This is technically feasible, but notoriously difficult to sustain – especially where busy stations cause extended platform dwell times. The two-platform terminus at Brixton would also be unworkable, and various schemes – mostly involving a single-track loop extension to Herne Hill – have been explored to overcome the problem.

An alternative to pushing frequencies to the limits is to increase the capacity of the trains themselves. The Underground's engineers are examining the concept of a train configured to make better use of the available tunnel diameter, lowering the floor and providing more gangway space than the 'D' stock, itself much larger than tube trains. The concept has aptly been called 'Space train', and gaps between cars would be eliminated by using short articulated segments to provide one continuous space instead of individual carriages. Doorways would be wider and optimally spaced for passenger flow and comfort, rather than the location dictated as now by the intrusion of wheels and other equipment into the saloon. Each train could carry up to around 50 per cent more people than 1967 stock in greater comfort: a vital by-product would be the virtual elimination of platform gaps as the short body section snaked around curves. The lower body would open up the possibility of using overhead power supply, with many operational and safety advantages over today's system.

Whatever solution is found for the Victoria line, the next tube for upgrading is the Piccadilly, where even with the interim improvements, capacity will fall short of demand. Much of the signalling will also be ready for renewal by 2010, and although the trains will by then be a little short of their potential years, the sheer mileage they run (currently 40 per cent more than other lines) means that replacement would not be premature. It is anticipated that peak frequencies of up to 34-36 trains per hour would be achieved following upgrade.

Options for the subsurface network are more diverse than the tube lines, as there is scope for altering routes and connecting to the National rail system if the benefits to London's travellers are significant. The intention is to resignal to the new standard of 34 tph on the trunk sections, and to replace existing trains with stock offering a standard bodyshell and equipment, but with door and seating configurations varied to suit the very different markets served. Such trains would require less development than highly specialist tube stock, and world class suppliers are already able to offer near standard packages which could be adapted. Because of the widely varying age and condition of the lines it will be necessary to phase the introduction of this strategy, but an early development could be to extend the platforms on the west side of the Circle line to allow train capacity to increase in key areas.

The Bakerloo has relatively modern signalling, and is currently more easily able to satisfy projected demand than other lines, and is thus slotted in at the end of the current programme for major enhancement around 2015-20. The trains themselves would be over 40 years old by then, but this is not envisaged as a problem.

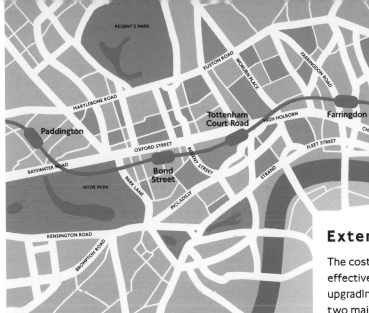

Station relief

Unless current forecasts prove to be wildly optimistic, over the next few years better train services are going to be delivering ever more customers to already crowded stations. Some improvement is possible by improved station management techniques, removing obstructions and clutter, increasing off-station ticket sales, providing better information and improving the regularity of the train service – though each of these measures also increases the number of people willing to travel. An intermediate level of relief comes from widening or adding a few subways, but more dramatic work will be needed at some locations.

Some of the more urgent stations are Knightsbridge, where work started in 1999, Russell Square, Camden Town (where increasing popularity of the local markets has increased demand by 17 per cent in five years), Heathrow 123, Covent Garden, Finsbury Park, King's Cross, Tottenham Court Road, Leicester Square (the busiest late evening station), Brixton and Wembley Park. Detailed plans exist for all of these, and some are virtually ready to proceed, but uncertainty still exists over funding availability. One further station requiring a near total rebuild is Hounslow East, with very unsatisfactory facilities for passengers, especially those heading for Heathrow. Plans for a very attractive new ticket hall and platform access have been completed, but again no funding is immediately available.

Other stations not mentioned still have severe capacity problems: examples are Oxford Circus, Holborn and Victoria, but expansion of these would have major property implications and thus be very expensive – it has been estimated that to give Victoria the space of, say, North Greenwich, would cost in the region of £250million.

Extending the System

The cost of new construction and scope for increasing the effectiveness of the existing system rightly dictate that upgrading today's railway has priority, but London also has two major rail schemes in mind, each involving the boring of large diameter tunnels across the centre of the city. The first is due to be CrossRail, connecting Paddington with Liverpool Street and allowing 12-car National rail trains to progress between the two termini and beyond (Reading and Heathrow to the west, perhaps Shenfield to the east) by way of Farringdon, Tottenham Court Road and Bond Street. The stations would be massive by current standards. The scheme was promoted in the early 1990s, but fell foul of Parliamentary indifference, cash shortage and the distraction of the privatisation and fragmentation of British Rail, the Underground's partner in the scheme at that time. The positive impact on London's economy makes this project very highly desirable.

The second scheme is for a south west-north east link joining the Fulham/Putney area in the south to Chelsea, Victoria, Piccadilly Circus, Tottenham Court Road, King's Cross and thence outwards to Hackney and either Epping (instead of the Central line) or Stratford and Docklands. The line would have surface-size trains, and would serve places currently without good rail connections, especially the deprived Hackney area, whilst relieving overcrowded lines in the centre of town. Funding problems are likely to delay work starting for many years.

Authority already exists to extend the East London line at both ends, towards Hackney and Dalston in the north (with the possibility of continuing to Highbury, with its useful connections) and towards Peckham and Dulwich in the south. Discussions between LT and Railtrack started in summer 1999 to develop services over these routes as part of Railtrack's proposal to maintain the subsurface lines. Again, development awaits funding but the value of the line, with its river crossing, to the National rail network could encourage imaginative services around London.

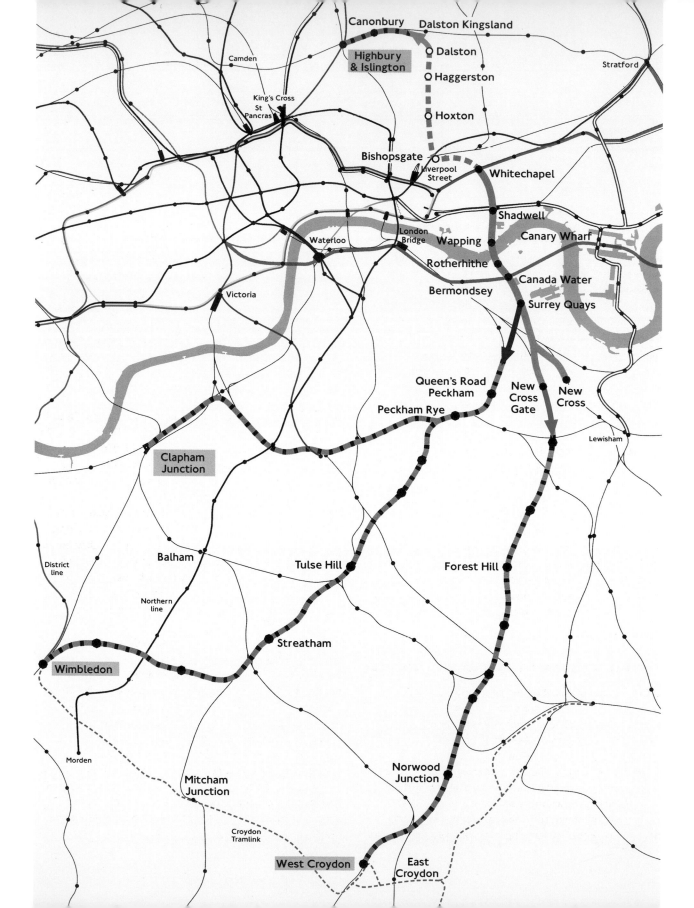

Canonbury   Dalston Kingsland

Camden

Stratford

Highbury
& Islington

○ Dalston

○ Haggerston

King's Cross
St Pancras

○ Hoxton

Bishopsgate   ○

Liverpool
Street

Whitechapel

Shadwell

Waterloo

London
Bridge

Wapping

Canary Wharf

Rotherhithe

Canada Water

Bermondsey

Victoria

Surrey Quays

Queen's Road
Peckham

New
Cross
Gate

New
Cross

Peckham Rye

Lewisham

Clapham
Junction

District
line

Balham

Tulse Hill

Forest Hill

Northern
line

Streatham

Wimbledon

Morden

Norwood
Junction

Mitcham
Junction

Croydon
Tramlink

West Croydon

East
Croydon

Left Map showing planned extension of the East London line from Whitechapel to Highbury & Islington and possible extensions south over main line railway routes.

Right Artist's impression of a hotel development planned above Southwark station.

Currently in the process of seeking authority is the proposed extension of the Piccadilly line to the intended new Terminal 5 at Heathrow Airport. This development followed the East London line through the process of a Transport & Works Act (TWA) application, made in November 1994 and which, unlike the old Parliamentary process it replaced, involves a Public Inquiry. Because the construction of the new terminal itself had to go through a Public Inquiry, it was sensibly decided to roll the two railway applications (Piccadilly line and Heathrow Express) into the same process. The level of opposition to the terminal building made this Inquiry the longest ever known in Britain, and did not conclude until March 1999. It is expected that the consequential report will not be ready until 2001, which renders it very unlikely that if approved the terminal, and the two railways, could be open before the end of 2006.

The final expansion scheme, currently on hold, is the linking of the Metropolitan line to Railtrack's Croxley Green branch near Watford. The two lines are only about 200 metres apart, although topography precludes a simple connection. This would give the Metropolitan access to central Watford instead of the quiet housing estates it currently reaches, and offer good ongoing connections to the National rail network and buses. The scheme remains alive, but no date is yet predicted for it to proceed to seek authority.

Property/Commercial Exploitation

With a number of valuable land sites, and 2.8 million journeys on the Underground each day, it is not surprising that it is possible to supplement fares income by small but significant revenue from advertising, property letting, and even using the railway as a film set.

Advertising on the Underground is legendary – once adverts were plastered on almost any available surface. Now the sites used are more selective, but the adverts themselves are often renowned for creative excellence. Innovative forms of advertising have followed, sometimes with stations sponsored under long term contracts (Capital Radio at Leicester Square and Xfm Radio at Camden Town). Trains have also been sponsored, the first in advertising livery being on the Piccadilly (United Airlines) and Circle (Yellow Pages). One Piccadilly line train had grab handles in the form of Vaseline deodorant pots.

The preference now, though, is for developments which positively improve facilities for customers, such as shops, coffee bars and Bank ATMs (cashpoints). In 1999 distribution started of a free morning newspaper at all Underground stations, London's first morning paper for very many years. Called 'Metro', and based on successful practice in Stockholm, each edition includes a page dedicated to London Transport matters.

More lucrative are the large property deals possible at a few sites. These can bring tremendous social and economic benefit as well as raising revenue. In recent years major developments have taken place at Bond Street, High Street Kensington, Hammersmith and most recently Finchley Road. Plans are well advanced for a very large development between Shepherd's Bush and White City, and to replace the run down property at South Kensington. Other developments being considered include some further major schemes at central London sites, but also the possibility of hotels at certain outer suburban stations, with the first aimed at Cockfosters, Hillingdon, Northolt and Hounslow West.

Chronologies

Present station names have been used in the list. Lines are shown in the order of opening.

Metropolitan and Hammersmith & City lines (including north half of Circle line)

1863 Opened on 10 January as the Metropolitan Railway from Farringdon to Paddington
1864 Extension to Hammersmith with branch from Latimer Road to Kensington (Olympia)
1865 Extension from Farringdon to Moorgate
1868 Branch opened from Baker Street to Swiss Cottage
1868 Part of Circle line opened from Edgware Road to South Kensington
1875 Extension from Moorgate to Liverpool Street
1876 Extension from Liverpool Street to Aldgate
1877 Service opened between Goldhawk Road and Richmond, over District Railway route between Ravenscourt Park and Richmond
1879 Extension from Swiss Cottage to Willesden Green
1880 Extension from Willesden Green to Harrow-on-the-Hill
1882 Extension from Aldgate to Tower Hill
1884 Branch opened from Aldgate East to East London Railway
1885 Extension from Harrow-on-the-Hill to Pinner
1887 Extension from Pinner to Rickmansworth
1889 Extension from Rickmansworth to Chalfont & Latimer and Chesham
1892 Extension from Chalfont & Latimer to Aylesbury
1894 Extension from Aylesbury to Verney Junction
1899 Branch to Brill taken over
1904 Branch opened from Harrow-on-the-Hill to Uxbridge
1906 Services from Goldhawk Road to Richmond withdrawn
1906 Through services to East London Railway withdrawn
1908 Extension from Aldgate East to Whitechapel
1913 Through services to East London Railway re-introduced
1925 Branch opened from Moor Park and Rickmansworth to Watford
1932 Branch opened from Wembley Park to Stanmore

1935 Closure of Brill Branch
1936 All services north of Aylesbury withdrawn (limited service re-introduced between Aylesbury and Quainton Road from 1943 to 1948)
1936 Extension from Whitechapel to Barking
1939 Through services to East London line withdrawn
1939 Transfer of Stanmore branch to the Bakerloo line
1940 Closure of branch from Latimer Road to Olympia
1961 Withdrawn between Amersham and Aylesbury upon electrification of the line between Rickmansworth and Amersham

District line (including south half of Circle line)

1868 Opened on 24 December as the Metropolitan District Railway between South Kensington and Westminster
1869 Branch opened from Gloucester Road to West Brompton
1870 Extension from Westminster to Blackfriars
1871 Extension from Blackfriars to Mansion House
1871 Branch opened from High Street Kensington to Earl's Court
1874 Extension from Earl's Court to Hammersmith
1877 Extension from Hammersmith to Richmond, over London & South Western Railway route between Ravenscourt Park and Richmond
1879 Branch opened from Turnham Green to Ealing Broadway
1880 Extension from West Brompton to Putney Bridge
1883 Branch opened from Acton Town to Hounslow Town
1883 Extension from Ealing Broadway to Windsor over Great Western Railway route
1884 Re-routed from west of Osterley to a new terminus at Hounslow West
1884 Extension from Mansion House to Whitechapel and East London Railway; completion of the Inner Circle (Circle line)

1885 Service between Ealing Broadway and Windsor withdrawn
1889 Extension from Putney Bridge to Wimbledon over London & South Western Railway route
1902 Extension from Whitechapel to Upminster (over London, Tilbury & Southend Railway route from Bromley-by-Bow to Upminster)
1903 Branch opened from Ealing Common to South Harrow
1905 Branch opened from Acton Town to South Acton
1905 Through services on East London Railway withdrawn
1910 Extension from South Harrow to Uxbridge
1910 Some journeys extended to Southend-on-Sea and, shortly after, to Shoeburyness, over London, Tilbury & Southend Railway route
1933 Services on Uxbridge branch withdrawn (taken over by Piccadilly line)
1939 Journeys to Southend and Shoeburyness withdrawn
1946 Services introduced between High Street Kensington and Olympia
1959 Closure of South Acton branch
1964 Service withdrawn between Acton Town and Hounslow West (covered by Piccadilly line, with which the section had been shared).

East London line

1869 Opened on 7 December as the East London Railway from Wapping to New Cross Gate
1876 Extension from Wapping to Liverpool Street (Great Eastern Railway)
1880 Branch opened from Surrey Quays to New Cross
1913 New Cross/New Cross Gate to Shoreditch section taken over by Metropolitan upon electrification of the line. No Metropolitan services beyond Shoreditch
1995 Closed for reconstruction of Thames Tunnel
1998 Reopened

Northern line

1890 City & South London Railway opened on 18 December between Stockwell and King William Street (near Bank)
1900 Extension north to Moorgate with new station at Bank and south from Stockwell to Clapham Common
1901 Extension from Moorgate to Angel
1907 Charing Cross, Euston & Hampstead Railway opened between Charing Cross and Golders Green with branch from Camden Town to Archway
1907 City & South London Railway extended from Angel to Euston
1914 Extension from Charing Cross to Embankment
1923 Extension from Golders Green to Hendon Central
1924 Extension from Hendon Central to Edgware and from Euston to Camden Town
1926 Extension from Clapham Common to Morden and from Embankment to Kennington
1939 Extension from Archway to East Finchley
1940 Extension from East Finchley to High Barnet over LNER route
1941 Branch opened to Mill Hill East over LNER route

Waterloo & City line

1898 Opened on 8 August as the Waterloo & City Railway between Waterloo and Bank
1994 Ownership of line transferred to London Underground

Central line

1900 Opened on 30 July as the Central London Railway between Shepherd's Bush and Bank
1908 Extension from Shepherd's Bush to Wood Lane (near White City)
1912 Extension from Bank to Liverpool Street
1920 Extension from Wood Lane to Ealing Broadway over GWR route

1946 Extension from Liverpool Street to Stratford
1947 Extension from Stratford to Newbury Park and
Woodford, partly over Great Eastern Railway routes
1947 Branch opened from North Acton to Greenford over
Great Western Railway route
1948 Extension from Greenford to West Ruislip over Great
Western Railway route
1948 Extension from Newbury Park to Hainault and from
Woodford to Hainault and Loughton over Great
Eastern Railway routes
1949 Extension from Loughton to Epping over Great
Eastern Railway routes
1957 Shuttle service between Epping and Ongar taken over
from BR upon electrification (closed 1994)

Bakerloo line

1906 Opened on 10 March as the Baker Street & Waterloo
Railway between Baker Street and Lambeth North;
extended to Elephant & Castle on 5 August
1907 Extension from Baker Street to Edgware Road
1913 Extension from Edgware Road to Paddington
1915 Extension from Paddington to Willesden Junction,
over London & North Western Railway route
between Queen's Park and Willesden Junction
1917 Extension from Willesden Junction to Watford
Junction over LNWR route
1939 Branch opened from Baker Street to Stanmore, over
Metropolitan line route between Finchley Road
and Stanmore
1979 Baker Street to Stanmore branch transferred to
Jubilee line
1982 Closure of section between Stonebridge Park and
Watford Junction
1984 Service restored between Stonebridge Park and
Harrow & Wealdstone

Piccadilly line

1906 Great Northern, Piccadilly & Brompton Railway
opened on 15 December between Hammersmith
and Finsbury Park
1907 Branch opened from Holborn to Aldwych
1932 Extension from Hammersmith to South Harrow over
District Railway route
1932 Extension from Finsbury Park to Arnos Grove
1933 Extension from Acton Town to Hounslow West over
District Railway route
1933 Extension from South Harrow to Uxbridge over
District Railway route
1933 Extension from Arnos Grove to Cockfosters
1975 Extension from Hounslow West to Hatton Cross
1977 Extension from Hatton Cross to Heathrow
1986 Single track loop extension at Heathrow to serve
Terminal 4
1994 Branch to Aldwych closed

Victoria line

1968 Opened on 1 September between Walthamstow
Central and Highbury & Islington; extended to
Warren Street on 1 December
1969 Extension from Warren Street to Victoria
1971 Extension from Victoria to Brixton

Jubilee line

1979 Opened on 1 May between Charing Cross and
Stanmore, over Bakerloo line route between Baker
Street and Stanmore
1999 Extension opened in stages from Green Park to
Stratford; closure of Charing Cross to Jubilee line
services